"*That's on Me* provides leaders the opportunity to learn from the mistakes and insights of others and then to reflect on their personal leadership style to avoid the same pitfalls. Strengthen your own leadership by applying the rich principles in this book!"

—**DEE ANN TURNER,** vice president (retired), Chick-fil-A, Inc., and best-selling author of *It's My Pleasure: The Impact of Extraordinary Talent and a Compelling Culture*

"*That's on Me* reminds us that leadership is a journey marked with many opportunities to submit our egos to a better way: the learning way. When leaders learn from their mistakes, our teams win, our organizations win, our families win . . . and the leader wins."

—**MICHAEL LECHTENBERGER,** chief information officer, Mutual of Omaha

"Most business books recycle the same idea over and over for 200 pages and aren't interesting to read. Not the case with *That's on Me*! I truly enjoyed reading this book. I already have several ideas for new things I want to try as a result of reading this book—I highly recommend!"

—**LIZ CASTRO,** senior vice president of human resources, The Krusteaz Company

"Mike McHargue hits the mark. Each of the five mistakes he highlights in *That's on Me* affects the overall culture of the workplace, productivity, and commitment at all levels of the organization. I recommend this book for any leader."

—**DAN MCNAMARA,** senior vice president and general manager, AMD Corporation

"Mike McHargue has a done a masterful job of interweaving his expertise with first-person accounts from seasoned executives across a wide variety of industries. Their stories significantly enhance the reader's understanding of the principles contained in the book and accelerate their practical application."

—**REID STEPHAN,** vice president and chief information officer, St. Luke's Health System

"Reading this book was a revelation; as a leader, I found solace in knowing I wasn't alone in navigating the complexities of business. The vulnerability and honesty of the business leaders' stories provided invaluable insights, inspiring me to learn from my own mistakes and take actionable steps toward improvement."

—STEVE MARTINEZ, owner and president,
Tradewinds General Contracting

"A great diamond takes time to form. There are no shortcuts. The same could be said of great managers. Now, with Mike McHargue's *That's on Me*, we can all shorten our path to becoming the leaders we've always wanted to be."

—NATALIE PICCOLA, owner and president, The Diamond Girls

"Mike McHargue speaks to the deepest human connections that leadership can forge—engaging values and vulnerability, expressing gratitude and affirmation, resolving conflict, and inspiring change."

—FATHER GERDENIO MANUEL, SJ, clinical psychologist and professor emeritus, University of San Francisco St. Ignatius Institute

"*That's on Me* is an essential guide for leaders. The candid, real-life parables have practical and scalable insights for building a healthy organization based on accessible principles."

—CARLOS DEVITIS, lead pastor, Eastwind Community Church

"This book serves as a crucial reminder of the essential principles and priorities of effective leadership. It dives into the art of building synergy within a team, providing clarity as a leader, and the importance of embodying your company's core values. It is an invaluable guide for those aspiring to lead with integrity and make an enduring impact."

—JERET WHITESCARVER, executive vice president, ESI

"Simply organized and easy to read, the stories and lessons learned in this book apply to civilian and military leaders alike. Whether a seasoned leader willing to self-reflect and improve or a new leader seeking guidance through common leadership mistakes, *That's on Me* hits the mark."

—JOSH LUCK, lieutenant colonel, USMC (retired); vice president of training operations, Quanta Services

"As a football coach, I've learned that making mistakes is inevitable, but learning from them is optional. This book is filled with opportunities to learn. The stories shared by these leaders prove that we are all fallible, yet give us hope that we can continue to grow and produce great things."

—IAN SMART, head football coach, Timberline High School

"When it comes to leadership, we're all rookies. Reading this will be a gift to not just you, but also to your team."

—JOHN ORTBERG, author, founder of BecomeNew.com

"Leadership mistakes are inevitable. *That's on Me* helps highlight the most common mistakes that can cause teams to be dysfunctional and well-intentioned work to go off the tracks. This is a must-read for leaders wanting to avoid these common mistakes."

—ROBERT (BOB) MILLER, former CEO and chairman emeritus, Albertsons Companies

"Savvy and novice leaders alike will benefit from *That's on Me*. No matter what kind of leader you are, you will find yourself in one (or more!) of these stories and will appreciate this advice setting you on the right path."

—AARON HOWELL, founder and former president, Northwest Lineman College

"McHargue leverages classic examples from proven leaders to reinforce organizational health concepts. All leaders, new and experienced, can gain a tremendous amount from these five missteps and how to avoid them."

—JEFF FEELER, former chairman, president, and CEO, US Ecology, Inc.

"While reading my copy of *That's on Me*, I was immediately able to apply one of its many lessons to an issue with a new member of our team. I would recommend this book to any leader looking to improve their skills or the health of their team."

—BEN BLEDSOE, president and CEO, Consumer Direct Care Network

"The short stories in *That's on Me* are designed to get the leader thinking about the way they lead and how they set the tone for their organization."

—RYAN CANTRELL, chief deputy superintendent,
Idaho State Department of Education

"When I worked with Mike McHargue, he never pretended to be the perfect leader and admitted his mistakes. That's part of what made him such an effective leader and what makes this book so valuable."

—ANDY PEDERSON, vice president of enterprise sales, Included Health

"A compassionate and empathetic leader, Mike McHargue is the exact right person to encourage leaders to avoid common mistakes. *That's on Me* will inspire you to think big on your path to becoming a better leader."

—MICALEA BREBER, talent solutions sales leader, LinkedIn

"Throughout my career in the navy, and then in consulting and sales leadership, I endured, observed, and made most of the mistakes highlighted in this book. Regardless of your profession or career stage, you will find something in *That's on Me* that resonates."

—KEVIN DUFFER, founder, KLD Consulting; director, federal sales, Udacity

"I have literally given hundreds of copies of Mike McHargue's original book, *Rookie Mistakes*, to my many clients. The key lessons in leadership are articulated in a way that are both compelling and useful. *That's on Me* is an even finer work that will appeal to the full range of company leadership."

—AL AMADOR, president, Amador Consulting;
principal consultant, The Table Group

"The common thread of vulnerability and ownership from the countless leaders throughout *That's on Me* reflects the mindset of every successful competitor I've battled against or with. This fast and impactful read is both thought provoking and inspiring. I couldn't put it down."

—DAN O'BRIEN, founder, Ten90 Consulting Group; principal consultant,
The Table Group; leadership development coach, Cincinnati Reds

"I wish I would have read and applied the principles from this book twenty-five plus years ago when beginning my leadership journey. Unfortunately, I've made all five of these leadership mistakes. Leaders who take these principles to heart and apply them will amplify their leadership effectiveness."

—DAVID HOYT, president and founder, The Principal
Group; principal consultant, The Table Group

"Humility leads to wisdom. In *That's on Me*, McHargue shares leaders' stories of humility, allowing you to gain practical wisdom from their mistakes. Reading this book will not only entertain you; it will improve you."

—BILL WEINGARTNER, founder, Bill Weingartner Consulting;
principal consultant, The Table Group

"*That's on Me* is an absolute masterclass on how we can learn from the mistakes of other leaders. The quick and engaging stories will challenge you to reflect and redefine your leadership style for the betterment of you and the people you lead."

—CASEY THOMPSON, founder, Casey Thompson
Consulting; principal consultant, The Table Group

"They say we learn more from our failures than our successes. Save yourself a tremendous amount of time and trouble by learning from others' mistakes first. *That's on Me* should be required reading at every business school across the country!"

–NEIL SULLIVAN, CEO, The Leadership Connection;
principal consultant, The Table Group

"From my experience, a leader's greatest influence comes through humility and a willingness to be known. These real-life, bite-sized leadership reflections offer the kind of wisdom my clients will take to heart and put into practice. Great read!"

–WALDEMAR KOHL, founder, Kohl Consulting;
principal consultant, The Table Group

"In this book, Mike McHargue has shown us dozens of ways we can become better leaders. The magic, however, is that the vulnerability of the leaders in this book also allows us to learn so many incredible lessons!"

–JAMES FELTON, president, Felton Consulting Group;
principal consultant, The Table Group

"In reading Mike's book, I'm realizing leaders consistently step into the same holes and stub their toes on the same hard edges. Thanks for pointing out these especially painful ones so we can all avoid them!"

–KEITH HADLEY, founder, Keith Hadley Consulting;
principal consultant, The Table Group

"Mike's well-curated collection of stories from successful leaders who have learned from their mistakes will challenge all of us to be more vulnerable and open with our teams. It's an eye-opener all leaders should read!"

–JEFF GIBSON, founder and president, Gibson
Consulting Group; principal consultant, The Table Group

"I love how Mike has captured stories that promote one of the most significant yet rarely adopted behaviors in leadership: vulnerability. Mistakes happen, but vulnerable leaders learn from them and set their people up for success."

—HRISHI BASKARAN, president, Ten Talent Group, LLC; principal consultant, The Table Group

"To acknowledge a mistake is one of the best displays of vulnerability in leadership. Mike's book is a celebration of that vulnerability, with some incredible leadership tips along the way. No leader, no human, can avoid mistakes, but we sure can learn from them."

—GLENN LYDAY, founder, Glenn Lyday Consulting; principal consultant, The Table Group

"With *That's on Me*, Mike has struck a balance few authors can achieve: presenting practical and relevant concepts that are timeless and profound. Every one of my CEO clients will be receiving this book as required reading."

—KEVIN TWOMEY, founder, Twomey Consulting; principal consultant, The Table Group

"From beginning to end, *That's on Me* offers bite-sized, easy-to-digest stories and practical advice that all leaders can immediately put into practice."

—RICK PACKER, CEO, The Packer Group; principal consultant, The Table Group

"In the footsteps of the greatest storyteller ever, Jesus, Mike's collections of veterans sharing principles for leadership success could hardly be more richly illustrated than they are in this volume. If ever there were a story-laden, do-it-yourself user manual to take yourself from rookie to pro, this is it."

—DANIEL MASSICK, president and founder, Massick Consulting; principal consultant, The Table Group

THAT'S
ON ME

THAT'S ON ME

SEASONED EXECUTIVES
CONFESS THEIR ROOKIE MISTAKES

MIKE McHARGUE

GREENLEAF
BOOK GROUP PRESS

Published by Greenleaf Book Group Press
Austin, Texas
www.gbgpress.com

Distributed by Greenleaf Book Group

For ordering information or special discounts for bulk purchases, please contact Greenleaf Book Group at PO Box 91869, Austin, TX 78709, 512.891.6100.

Design and composition by Greenleaf Book Group
Cover design by Greenleaf Book Group
Cover Images from Adobe Stock

Publisher's Cataloging-in-Publication data is available.

Print ISBN: 979-8-88645-277-8

eBook ISBN: 979-8-88645-278-5

To offset the number of trees consumed in the printing of our books, Greenleaf donates a portion of the proceeds from each printing to the Arbor Day Foundation. Greenleaf Book Group has replaced over 50,000 trees since 2007.

Printed in the United States of America on acid-free paper

24 25 26 27 28 29 30 31   10 9 8 7 6 5 4 3 2 1

First Edition

To my wife, Anna, for your amazing grace
during 30 years of my mistakes.

And, to my kids, Elena, Jack, and Gabriella—go fast,
take chances, and learn from your mistakes.
Because you know where whiners go . . .

CONTENTS

FOREWORD

——

Rookies are prone to mistakes, and we expect that. Veterans are prone to mistakes, and we are surprised by that. What Mike McHargue has done in *That's on Me: Seasoned Executives Confess Their Rookie Mistakes* is provide a primer and a reminder all in one. What's particularly effective about what he's done here is that he gives leaders colorful and practical advice, and then reinforces that advice through the experiences of leaders who are humble enough to tell their stories.

A new leader needs wisdom, but in this age of ubiquitous information, it has become a great challenge to sift through everything that is out there and come up with something that is both relevant and digestible. McHargue has done just that. He has curated the insights he has gained in his consulting with a fascinating mix of leaders from a wide variety of fields—people who have made mistakes, learned from them, and want to help others avoid some of their missteps.

Beyond the wisdom of the concepts and stories, McHargue is a masterful communicator, combining practical insights with humor. *That's on Me* is not only a readable and useful book, but it should also be a resource for leaders who want access to just-in-time advice when they are staring squarely at a situation that has the potential for success or failure. So, read the advice here, and keep it handy. Even if you're a rookie, one day soon you'll be seen as a veteran, and you'll recognize that no one is immune from the occasional mistakes that are part of having the courage to be a leader.

Patrick Lencioni

Founder and CEO, The Table Group

Best-Selling Business Author

AUTHOR'S NOTE

———

"What's the biggest mistake you have ever made as a leader?" and "How did it affect the people in your organization?" are questions I started asking teams soon after starting my business working with executive leaders. The stories were rich, and the leaders were open and vulnerable in sharing them. It gave me an idea for a book—this book.

At the time, I had been married for 20 years to my amazing wife, who is also an amazing book editor. And for most of those years, I *really* wanted to write a book. I had everything one needs to write a book at my disposal, except one thing: an author smart or expert enough about any topic to offer something meaningful to the world. Well, it turns out I am an expert in one thing after all: making mistakes. I feel like I have made them *all* during my career leading people and teams. So that's the focus of this work, organized into five sections.

But why five?

I have heard it said that three is a magic number. There is small, medium, and large. Gold, silver, and bronze. Red, yellow, and green. But I would argue that a better, more complete number is five.

Five is the number of aspiration. It's a five-star hotel, restaurant, or theater production. It is the highest ranking on a team assessment. It is the exact right amount—a handful. (And, really, who doesn't love a high-five?) According to team management expert Patrick Lencioni, it's the number of dysfunctions that can keep a team from reaching its potential, but it is also a great size for a team: large enough for diversity, but small enough to be agile and execute with speed.

And as we try to recall things to our mind, five things come easily.

Written with all of this in mind, *That's on Me: Seasoned Executives Confess Their Rookie Mistakes* fully embraces this aspirational number: five chapters (mistakes) with five stories each (and now with two additional stories for good measure). Easy to remember. Easy to apply.

It is my hope that these five chapters offer something you can use as you strive to become the best leader you can be.

INTRODUCTION

Throughout my career, both in technology organizations and now as a principal consultant focused on the organizational health movement, I have seen experienced executives and rookie leaders alike make the same leadership mistakes over and over. In fact, I made many of those same mistakes both as a junior leader and sometimes now as a veteran leader. But I can say with conviction that many of my errors could have been avoided, had a seasoned executive or two (or in this case, 35) offered a little advice or shared a relevant experience as I chartered those new leadership waters.

I remember the day I thought some of that guidance might come—one day about 25 years ago, when the CEO called me into his office unexpectedly.

I had just started my career in management and was working as a sales manager for a software technology start-up in Silicon Valley. It was a great time to be in technology sales and a great time for start-ups—the heart of the dotcom run-up. With Y2K fears at their frenzied peak, breakthrough technologies being developed and productized, and new companies being formed daily in dorm rooms and coffee shops, there was a lot going on in that time and place in the technology world.

In the CEO's office already sat three additional members of his executive team, awaiting my arrival. This was going to be either really good or really bad! One of the executives shared that our company's senior sales leader was leaving to go to another start-up called "Gogle"—that's really what he said . . . Gogle! He wondered out loud why any person in their right mind would leave our great start-up for that little, oddly named company. (Last I heard that departing leader was living on an island somewhere—*his* island!)

The executive leaders had called me into the office, hoping I would consider taking over that significant leadership role in our organization. The role meant that I would not only join the senior executive team in leading the sales and support teams, but also take responsibility for all customer relationships across multiple geographies. I was flattered and excited, understandably nervous. Having never led such a large organization with multiple teams before, I asked what I'd need to do to be successful.

Those top executives collectively looked me in the eye and spent the next several hours sharing the specifics of the thoughtful plan they had jointly crafted specifically with my success and the success of the organization in mind. It included taking an assessment geared toward helping determine my strengths and weaknesses as a leader, as well as following a thorough development plan to help me grow in my new role. They had set aside a significant budget for classes and coaching I might need as I learned and crafted my skills as a world-class leader.

And best of all, each of them committed to taking personal interest in my success by setting aside time each week to mentor me. The intent of the mentoring was to provide guidance and a venue for open dialogue, and to help me learn from mistakes they had made or seen in the past. All this came with a generous pay package and an equity position, along with an all-expenses-paid trip with my wife to Tahiti to consider their offer.

I gave them each a big bear hug and left the office excited about what the future would hold.

Unfortunately, it didn't really happen that way.

These senior executives really *did* call me into the office and offer me the job that day. But there was no personally crafted plan and no assessment to gauge my readiness. There were no resources set aside to help me learn and grow, and definitely no commitment to meet with me and mentor me as I took on this role. The stories of the mistakes they made were never shared, and I was left to figure the job out on my own.

In response to my inquiry regarding how to be successful, one of them said, "It's really not that hard. Your team is selling more than all the other teams. Just have every team do what they do, and we'll be in great shape."

That was the extent of the training and coaching I received. So, armed with that minimal guidance—and that guidance alone—I was left to flounder through my first significant leadership role.

As a result of the lack of direction and support, and my "trial and error" approach to leadership, I made a lot of mistakes as a new leader. I cringe to think that most of those early errors could have been avoided, had I been offered even the most basic guidance. Some of the mistakes I made (and this is just a small sampling) include allowing confusion to reign in my organization by not being clearer about purpose and priorities; failing to admit my mistakes and apologize when I made them; failing to trust the people who worked for me to do their jobs; running truly awful meetings;

hiring too fast and firing too slow; and failing to give honest and direct feedback.

But I wasn't all bad. There were two things I did right, early and often throughout my career as a leader, that thankfully prevented even more errors. The first was to actively seek out guidance from leaders I respected. The guidance I received, both on things I should do as a leader and things I shouldn't do, often came in the form of stories. These stories brought the coaching to life, helping me grasp the importance of the guidance and how it might be applied to the teams I was leading. They also planted the seed that would one day grow into an idea for a book—this book.

The second thing I did right as a young leader was read every book I could find on the topic of leading teams and leading people. To be clear, I am not a voracious reader. My attention span is short, and my patience for long-winded theories and thoroughly explained research methodologies is minimal. That said, in my early career as a leader, I read (or more accurately, started to read) hundreds of books on this topic. But when all was said and done, the books that resonated with me most (and the ones I actually finished!) over those two decades were the fables written by Patrick Lencioni.

When I took on multiple sales teams, I read *The Five Dysfunctions of a Team*. After applying what I learned, two things happened. First, the teams started getting along better. And as nice as that was, the second outcome was even more important: My teams' results started to improve. Dramatically.

When I joined a company that was known for its terrible meetings, I read Lencioni's work *Death by Meeting* and applied what I learned across the division I led. Meetings improved because we were talking about the most important things and engaging in good debate; we made better decisions and ended each meeting with clarity. Productivity at those meetings increased, as it did across the company as the methodology was adopted across the enterprise.

Later in my career, when I took on responsibility for a consulting business unit in a different company, I read and applied the concepts from Lencioni's book *Getting Naked.* The result? Customer service scores improved, as did all of our other key performance indicators.

These books and others fueled my passion for improving teams and organizations and proved that a thoughtful, disciplined approach to applying simple concepts and ideas could dramatically improve organizational results.

After leading organizations and teams for the better part of two decades, I founded my own consulting business cleverly named Mike McHargue Consulting, and simultaneously aligned my business to The Table Group, a Patrick Lencioni company, working with that business as a principal consultant. This business and my role in it have afforded me the opportunity to work with hundreds of CEOs and other executive leaders and their teams over the past decade.

It turns out that those leaders also made mistakes.

The best leaders admit their mistakes so that others might learn from them. This makes everyone on the team and in the organization better. Perhaps that's why these 35 leaders agreed to share some of their stories here, including what they have learned from their oversights and missteps.

Whether you are a first-time manager or a seasoned executive wanting to hone your skills, I am hopeful that in these pages you'll find some wisdom to help you grow as a leader.

MISTAKE #1

Allowing Confusion

Clear is kind. Unclear is unkind.

—Brené Brown

ALLOWING CONFUSION

————

When I work with executive teams, early in the first day together, I often lead an interactive exercise called "best team," where I ask each executive to think about the best team they have ever been on. I ask that they be creative in thinking about teams outside of their current team and not limit their example to only business teams. Their best team could be within their current organization or with a previous employer, but could also be from a community organization, a school, a sports team, their church, or even their family.

I say, "Of all the teams you have been on, in all the organizations you have worked with or for, pick the *one* team that stands out as the very best. And why *that* team? What are the things that make that particular team rise above the dozens, if not hundreds, of other teams you have worked on or for?" I give them a few minutes to come up with that best team and to note the key qualities or characteristics that made that team so great.

After a minute or two of individual reflection, I typically pair them up and ask them to share their best team with their assigned partner. As the sharing begins, the energy in the room immediately grows exponentially. The member of the pair who is sharing the best team story sits up straighter and breaks into a smile. There is typically laughter and excitement in the room that weren't there previously.

Once a couple of minutes have passed, I ask them to switch roles, and again there is an energy surge as the second member of each pair begins to recall their very best team. As I try to move on from this part of the exercise, invariably the conversations continue, and I need to ask multiple times for the stories to stop so we can move on. Leaders like talking about their best teams!

I run this exercise for two reasons: to set the positive tone for our off-site event and, more important, to start making the business case for the importance of great teams and great teamwork.

Next, I spend a few minutes asking for a handful of volunteers to repeat their stories for the benefit of the group. I chart their shared comments regarding the characteristics and behaviors that made those teams so great.

More often than not, the first volunteer to share the best team story with the larger group shares that their best team was one where politics ran rampant; confusion reigned; and team members had absolutely no idea about the team's purpose, values, goals, or top priorities.

I kid.

Instead, the first to respond explains that their very best team had clarity of purpose in the organization or team, as well as clarity regarding values and appropriate behaviors. Goals and objectives were well defined and discussed often, and within those goals, the most important were both clear and repeated frequently by the leader to avoid confusion and a lack of team alignment.

As leaders, it is our job not only to establish clarity but to communicate that clarity, especially with respect to company purpose, values, and priorities. And we need to do that as often as possible. But if truth be told, many leaders are terrible at this.

Over the course of my career as a leader, I have been as bad about clarity as anyone. My work with leaders and their teams, though, has validated that I am not alone in some of the following weak (but honest) excuses for not communicating clarity:

- I didn't know the answers or wasn't clear myself.

- I was too busy to stop and share with my team or organization.

- I assumed the team (somehow magically!) already knew.

- I was embarrassed to repeat myself. I had smart people on my team and had told them once—surely they understood the message the first time!

These are embarrassing and inadequate reasons for allowing confusion as a leader. If you see yourself in any of these, however, you are in good company.

When my peers and I at The Table Group work with leaders and their teams, we strive to help our clients establish both behavioral alignment and intellectual alignment. Based on Patrick Lencioni's Second Discipline of Organizational Health, spelled out in *The Advantage*, we help teams answer the following six critical questions:

1. Why do we exist?
2. How will we behave?

3. What do we do?

4. How will we succeed?

5. What is most important, right now?

6. Who must do what?

The idea is that if a team can answer these questions, is perfectly aligned around those answers, and is in sync behaviorally as well, the organization is on a great path toward stronger organizational health—and results will follow.

So, the first mistake I address here concerns allowing confusion to reign in a leader's teams and organizations. What follows in this section are seven great leaders describing mistakes they made and advice they can share with respect to clarity in one's team or organization.

We begin with a story concerning the "why" of an organization—an organization's core purpose.

ALLOWING CONFUSION ABOUT PURPOSE

David Griffin, CEO, Griffin Media

Breaking News: Tornado Warning.
We interrupt our regularly scheduled programming
for this severe weather update.

These alerts are broadcasted regularly each year from our television stations in Tulsa and Oklahoma City, Oklahoma, in April, May, and June.

As those words are spoken by the meteorologists and news anchors who are front and center as the spokespeople for each unfolding weather event, a flurry of activity is already taking place in our stations and across the state. Our internal company messaging system deploys to our employees, notifying them to come into the station, although most are already on their way. It's all hands on deck.

Warning lights indicating breaking news are lighting up at our stations to notify all of the gravity of the situation and drive appropriate action. Storm chasers, news crews, and camera operators quickly depart and position themselves strategically but safely. This is a major weather event, and the people of our state are counting on us for timely, accurate information.

This is who we are, and this is our time.

Our company purpose is "to keep Oklahomans safe, informed, and entertained," and a crisis like this is a great and dramatic example of why we are in business. There is great clarity around this purpose, both on our leadership team and across the company.

But it wasn't always this way.

Our 114-year-old company was once divided into two distinct businesses: food manufacturing and a television station in Oklahoma City. Clearly, there was no synergy at all between those two. And even though both businesses were strong and profitable, they were very different in purpose and focus. This not only confused people in the organization and ownership, but also led to challenges for our leadership and their teams.

A critical point in our company's history came when we made the decision to identify the one business we wanted to be in, split off the other business (in this case, the food side), and articulate the purpose of our organization. We focused our energies on determining the purpose of the company and eventually crafted a message that our employees and constituents could endorse and appreciate. We believe our clear purpose is to keep Oklahomans safe, informed, and entertained.

Employees in every organization want to know the work they do has meaning. As the leadership team of our company, we take seriously our job to define our company's purpose and to make sure our employees understand that purpose. My senior leaders and I use the "safe, informed, and entertained" statement to open every presentation, both internally and externally, and talk about it regularly in meetings across our enterprise. It informs our strategy, helps guide our decision-making, and ensures we attract the right people to join our company.

I can't emphasize enough the importance of clearly identifying the business you are in, creating an accurate and clear purpose statement, and communicating that purpose regularly across your organization. Once my leaders and team recognized and embraced this strategy and purpose, it was much easier for us all to work together to achieve our mission of keeping our fellow Oklahomans safe, informed, and entertained.

ALLOWING CONFUSION ABOUT VALUES

Erik Peterson, former CEO, Corporate Visions, Inc.,
author of *The Three Value Conversations*

Twenty-five years ago, I received what I still consider the greatest honor of my professional career: the Founder's Award, given each year to the employee who best represented the company's values.

What made this award so special was that it was *not* bestowed by management. It was voted on by employees. Prior to the ceremony, everyone in the company submitted one name, and the person who got the most votes won the award.

I was not expecting that person to be me. I'd only been with the company a short time, and although we'd had a great year and I was excited to be there, it was my first year. I was just happy to be sitting there, watching from the audience as one person after another was called up on stage and recognized for various accomplishments.

The Founder's Award was the biggest honor, so it was the final award of the night. And they didn't announce the winner right away. The company founder built suspense by talking about the person who was being honored. When he finally did reveal my name, I was shocked. I somehow found myself on stage being handed a Rolex watch with an inscription on the back that read "Founder's Award Winner" and fumbling my way through a short acceptance speech.

I don't remember the actual words I spoke. What I remember is my wife in the audience, crying because it was such a special moment. I remember being surrounded by people—my peers—hugging and congratulating me. And I remember how overwhelming and moving the whole experience was.

After the ceremony, I went out with a group of colleagues to continue the celebration. At some quiet moment late in the evening, I found myself alone in a corner of the bar. I took off the watch to look at it again. I held it in my hands, then turned it over to reread the inscription. And as I sat there looking at the words "Founder's Award Winner," it suddenly struck me that even though my fellow employees had voted me most worthy of winning this award, and even though that meant I was the person who best represented the company's values, I had *no earthly idea what any of those values were.*

I knew there were six values, because I had been told there were six values.

I knew one was probably *teamwork*, because that's always a value.

I knew one must have been *vision*, because I remembered a poster up on a wall somewhere of a person looking across an ocean, so of course that must have represented vision, right?

But I had no idea what any of the other values were. And that's because, during that entire year when I was supposedly embodying them, those values—whatever they were—never influenced a single decision I'd made. There was no point at which I said to myself, *I've got to make this tough decision. What do the company values tell me I should do?*

Then I reflected on the effort the founders must have put in to come up with those values. There had probably been a workshop at a retreat somewhere, where they spent several days putting all these values together in the hope they would help employees make better decisions. Yet there I was, the guy who'd won the award, and those values hadn't impacted my decisions at all.

That realization stuck with me for a long time. If you don't have a good way to communicate values, why have them? Values aren't supposed to be just a slogan. They're only important if they inform decision-making, and they can only be called "values" if you're willing to sacrifice some pretty big things to live by them. And if that's what you want your values to do, then they need to be something you can recall in the moments when you're making those tough decisions.

I told myself then that if I ever had the opportunity, I'd do a better job of getting those values across than our founders had.

Fast-forward 20 years. Now I was an executive in a different company, in a session with a consultant developing our company values. As the leadership team struggled through the exercises, listing the characteristics of our top employees and trying to translate those qualities into our core values, I felt an overpowering sense of déjà vu. Nobody outside that room knew the core values we expected them to live by. And anyway, if we were going to make those values work, it wasn't enough simply to *tell* people what our values were. We had to bring them to life, in a way they'd remember, so those values would be the first thing our people would call upon when faced with tough decisions.

Here's what we did.

We knew from our research that people remember stories better than words or slogans. So I talked to the entire company about our core values and shared real stories of team members living those values. Then senior leaders followed up on my company-wide presentation by meeting with smaller teams of employees to share their stories and solicit examples from their own teams.

The approach worked well. Because every employee not only heard about our core values but heard them communicated in a way that stuck, people were able to understand and act on them.

CEOs and other senior leaders must be the key champions and guardians of an organization's core values. They must talk about those values at every opportunity; use them in interviewing and recruiting; and be willing to lose money, if necessary, to honor them. And they must not hesitate to move people out of the business who do not respect or uphold them.

That's how values inform decision-making and guide behavior. And that's how they make our business stronger.

ALLOWING CONFUSION ABOUT GOALS

Dave Myers, CEO, Apex Leaders

Coronado High School in San Diego, California, has been known for its water polo teams for a long time. Anyone who cares about the sport has at least heard of this school, as it has won 17 regional championships and three state championships since 1999, has had consecutive representation on every US Olympic water polo team in the six Olympic games up to and including 2020, and has achieved a 100 percent acceptance rate into the US Navy SEALs program spanning multiple decades. No other school can claim that same success on *any* of those metrics, much less all of them.

Years ago, I was fortunate to be able to play for that team. During those precious high school years, though, I had no idea how the success of that team and the lessons I learned there would mold me as a future leader. I didn't fully understand the impact of putting team over self as we worked toward a common goal. I didn't recognize that success came when you combined hard work and the correct execution of small mechanics of the game, or that our wins and losses ultimately came from holding each other accountable for our actions and efforts.

After high school, I went on to play college water polo at the University of California, Berkeley. And while that team had a collection of amazing athletes, it didn't achieve anywhere near the same type of success our high school team had achieved. Our challenges as a team came alongside our relative lack of focus, a failure to put our shared goals above that of the individual, and limits to really holding one another accountable.

These failures followed me into the business world. Lack of focus and a misunderstanding about company goals and objectives were evident across many of the companies I served in my early career. Goals and objectives for individual team members were never as clear as they should have been, so no one was accountable for the company's misses or successes. Predictably and sadly, those companies had intermittent success; in most cases, they had great potential that was never realized.

When I look back on those organizations, especially where I had a leadership role, it's clear that *I* was part of the problem. It is a leader's job to create clarity around goals, get buy-in from the team, ensure accountability, and ultimately deliver results. As I crafted a business plan to launch my own company, Apex Leaders, I vowed not to follow that same pattern of poor focus, lack of understanding, and missed opportunity. I now take every opportunity—and make others do the same—to ensure that we have great clarity about the direction our company is headed.

Ten years ago at Apex Leaders, we developed a new process to ensure we are aligned in our thinking. First, we set three-year goals to lay out a big picture. We follow that with one-year goals, which are broken into quarterly 13-week "sprints" with designated individuals responsible for carrying a specific goal—what we call "rocks." Related to these rocks, we give very specific assignments to each team member, who is then responsible for seeing that commitments are met. Every rock is measured in a simple manner: red, yellow, or green. Asking, "What's our green on that?" is a concise way of asking what success would look like on a defined goal.

Daily monitoring of key metrics (via dashboards), together with weekly team meetings to review the prior week's progress on our three or four rocks for the quarter, creates friendly accountability; we make sure each rock receives the attention and focus it deserves. If a rock is in danger of not being met (color coded as red), it gets the extra attention and the resources it deserves in order to get back on track. And finally, to ensure we aren't overtaken by distractions, we tie bonuses to the accomplishment of each quarterly and annual goal. When it comes to setting goals, we've learned less is more—laser focus on a few key objectives is the trick. To select goals it truly wants to achieve, the team had to get comfortable saying "no" more often than it says "yes."

Using this new process, Apex Leaders consistently achieved its annual objectives and multiplied the business 10x over the next six years. We then set a subsequent goal to 10x the business in the next six years. While growing exponentially, the company has received annual community recognition for being one of the best places to work. I am convinced that none of this would have happened without the intense focus, alignment, and clarity around goals and objectives that my team and I live daily.

ALLOWING CONFUSION ABOUT THE TOP PRIORITY

Matt Wolff, President, St. Luke's Health Plan

The word *priority* comes from the Latin word *prior*, meaning "first": the one thing that comes before all others. And before the 20th century, that word was only singular in form—*priority* rather than *priorities*, which is a more common term in my experience in organizations. I am not an etymologist who studies words (nor an entomologist—that's about bugs), but I have become a passionate advocate for clarity around having a most important goal, a single priority—and a believer in the great impact that focus on a single goal can have on a leadership team and the organization for which it is accountable.

In Idaho, where my family and I make our home, great examples abound of people achieving great things by focusing on a singular priority. Coach Chris Peterson and the Boise State Broncos went 12–0 in the regular season and shocked the college football world with a win over the University of Oklahoma in the 2007 Fiesta Bowl—after setting the singular goal of winning a Bowl Championship Series game. Kristin Armstrong won three gold medals—each after setting her sights on earning that top spot on the podium in Beijing, London, and Rio de Janeiro, respectively.

In the Idaho-based cult film *Napoleon Dynamite*, Napoleon was able to help his friend Pedro secure the role of class president (*Vote for Pedro!*) after developing singular focus in their campaign, capped off with an electrifying dance that sealed the victory. And in emergency departments, clinics, and surgical operating rooms throughout the St. Luke's Health System, our skilled caregivers' singular focus on each patient helps improve the health of people in the communities we serve and saves lives every single day.

When I was hired to lead the in-organization health insurance company—St. Luke's Health Plan, a start-up—we were crystal clear about our purpose: "to connect people with affordable, hassle-free healthcare." But I should have taken a hint from these Idaho examples and other great leaders about the importance of focusing on one singular goal, and therein lay my mistake.

In the healthcare industry, a sense of urgency around whatever is right in front of you, such as stopping the bleeding or providing lifesaving measures, often takes precedence from a task perspective. That focus on the urgent often carries over to administrative matters as well, and that proved to be the case in our new organization. With so many things to do as we started our business—hiring the right team, securing a license from the state, meeting compliance requirements, identifying partnerships, building systems, gaining board and executive approvals, securing and managing the budget, and so forth—our team became overly reactive. Meetings became more about fighting fires and addressing the pressing issues in front of us than about focusing on our longer-term success and what really mattered most.

Only when we agreed upon and built out our thematic goal—the rallying cry for our executive team and therefore our organization—did we get the alignment and momentum we needed to be successful as we launched our business. We titled the goal *Members On!*

The focus was to align around acquiring and serving our first members (customers) within the time parameter that we had committed to with our board, our partners, each other, and the rest of our employees. Having collectively built the thorough, detailed plan, each executive team member knew their role in the shared goal and took personal responsibility for seeing that we were successful as we worked *together*. Our meetings became more focused and proactive. After starting each meeting with clarity with respect to our purpose and values, we used the time to check in on our thematic goal, our progress against it, and any obstacles that might be in the way of achieving it. If ever any part of the plan was in jeopardy, we would adjust our meeting agenda in real time. When something was truly our most important priority, it deserved immediate attention in both our weekly tactical meetings and our monthly operating meetings.

It has become my belief that great leaders and great teams always have absolute clarity about their most important goal, objectives, and key results. The priority goal should be singular, time-based, shared by the whole team, and discussed at every staff meeting. It is also my belief that alignment around that singular thematic goal is the best way to bring a team and an organization together. Our experience is that everyone wants to belong to a winning team focused on a common goal so that they are validated in knowing success.

Our latest (aggressive!) thematic goal is to "build a foundation to enable 25,000 members by the end of 2025." And when we achieve that goal, we will be simultaneously fulfilling our mission of connecting Idahoans with affordable, hassle-free healthcare.

ALLOWING CONFUSION ABOUT STRATEGY

Dennis Doan, Fire Chief, Gig Harbor Fire and Medic One

It was the evening of June 30, 2016, when I received an emergency notification from headquarters. My wife and I turned to each other and simultaneously said, "I smell fire." Duty was calling, and I had to get to the incident command post (ICP) immediately.

As I left home with appropriate urgency, my wife asked me—for the first of many times that evening—if she needed to evacuate. I told her to stay put, at least for now. As I drove away, I could see the line of fire in the foothills, approximately two miles from our house. The fire would become known as the Table Rock Fire and would eventually burn more than 2,500 acres in a five-hour period.

For the more than 300 people who made up our Boise Fire Department, where I was chief at the time, a fire in our hometown was always personal. In this instance the proximity to my home, family, and neighbors made this one all the more so.

When I arrived at the ICP, the battalion chief was leading the response and in command. It was a joint effort with the US Bureau of Land Management, an effort that would deploy more than 200 firefighters, 14 structure engines, 20 wildland engines, two hotshot crews, a dozer, and numerous air assets before the night was over. As per protocol, the battalion chief would command the effort from start to finish. My role was to support his work; provide guidance; aid in the big decisions as needed; and be the point person for informing the mayor, the city council, the public, and the media via interviews and regular, timely updates.

Decisions would need to be made quickly, and the stakes were high. As is often the case for our line of work, this was truly a matter of life or death.

With 50-mile-per-hour winds and the fire moving in the direction of thousands of foothills homes, a first and most critical decision was whether we would conduct a direct attack—aggressively fight the fire and shelter in place—or conduct an indirect attack by evacuating first and containing the fire second.

With limited time to make this critical decision, we looked to our three strategic priorities during a crisis like this:

1. Life safety
2. Incident stabilization
3. Property conservation

Using those priorities as strategic anchors to make the decision, we decided to aggressively fight the fire. This meant *not* evacuating.

In a fire crisis like this, you have to choose to go on offense *or* play defense—there isn't time or resources to do both. In taking the offensive strategy, we immediately put the men and women of our department in the actual line of the fire between the homes and the encroaching blaze. This strategy, and their great execution of the strategy, worked successfully: The fire was diverted around the homes in danger and was eventually put out completely.

It turned out to be the right decision. The evening had started with the potential of thousands of homes lost—and many lives lost as well. Once the fire was out, however, only two structures were lost and there were no human casualties.

I credit the success of this night to the brave men and women of our local department working in tandem with those of the Bureau of Land Management. Here's what enabled their success: The strategy was clear, the right decisions were made, and proper protocols were followed.

Obviously, a strategy is critical and must be clear when a crisis is at hand. But what about when the urgency is not so great, and life is not at risk? I would contend that strategy is critical then as well, although I must admit that I haven't always been as clear about strategy in nonemergency situations. Leaders shouldn't wait for a fire (a literal one or a figurative one) to know what's most important as decisions are made to ensure the organization's success.

ALLOWING CONFUSION BY UNDER-COMMUNICATING

Beth Toal, Vice President, Communications and Marketing, St. Luke's Health System

Of all people, I know the importance of sharing messages multiple times (research says at least seven!) before people actually internalize your point. Two of my primary responsibilities as vice president for communications and marketing for the largest healthcare system in Idaho are to articulate the mission of our organization—"to improve the health of the people in the communities we serve"—and to communicate our areas of focus as an organization and where we are making an impact. My department's role in the organization is to "communicate and activate the mission of St. Luke's," and that begins with consistent and clear external messaging.

So, how was it possible that I missed the mark in communicating and building understanding with my own team?

My team is extremely competent and professional, and many team members have worked together for years. At one point, however, I started to recognize that something was off. It felt like team members were working in silos, and it was becoming increasingly difficult to get things finished. I noticed a growing tension where there had been none before and found myself having to intervene more and more. Significant time in my meetings, and sometimes the better part of my day, was spent mediating misunderstandings and personal conflicts.

On top of that, when we would get together for leadership meetings and someone on the team would ask a question, I would be thinking, *Haven't we already had this conversation?* I couldn't figure out why things were no longer "clicking."

That's when the irony struck me. While my team and I were indeed doing a good job communicating *externally*, I assumed I was doing that same good job communicating *internally*. But that hadn't been the case. I was under-communicating with my internal team, and they needed more from me. They needed me to communicate clearly and constantly.

Once that realization became clear, I knew I couldn't simply close this gap with a one-time discussion. I needed to be intentional about *overcommunicating*. If I didn't add this intention, I would slip back into muscle memory and do exactly what I had been doing previously. My challenge was to ensure I didn't let that happen again. I didn't want to take for granted that we would figure things out without constant communication of a clear message about our focus, our priorities, and our values across the department.

After multiple conversations with my direct reports to create and reinforce clarity around the most important things, we held the first of what later became many department-wide meetings to clarify and reinforce our purpose, discuss living our values, plan together how we would succeed going forward, and communicate the top priorities in the department. We blew up our meeting structure and started over in designing how information and communication would flow. As a team, we committed to discussing the most important things with the right people in the right venues *at the right frequency*. We recognized our differences with respect to managing conflict and have used that new understanding to ensure healthy and constructive conversations. This, we believed, would ensure we didn't slip back into the old behaviors that resulted in the poor or ineffective communication that had plagued us.

Effective, clear communication took discipline as well as regular auditing and improvement to ensure this approach stayed effective for the team. As a result of our deliberate work in this area, my leaders and the rest of the department began performing again at their highest levels. Communication—indeed, overcommunication—began flowing up, down, and across the department, and achievement of our goals was now well within reach.

ALLOWING CONFUSION BY FAILING TO OVERCOMMUNICATE AND TO REINFORCE CLARITY

Dave Gillrie, CEO, Hoover Treated Wood Products

I am a long-suffering Detroit Lions fan. If you know anything about the Lions (or professional football in general), you know that's the only kind of Lions fan there is. I don't suspect they're the least successful team in professional sports history, but they are definitely in the conversation.

Seventeen playoff appearances since their inception in 1930. An overall record of 591–707–34 and a playoff record of 9–14 across those 94 years. Zero Super Bowl appearances. Dan Campbell, the current coach, is working hard to transform the team into a winning organization and to develop a winning culture. And it is working. The Lions are winning (at least for now). All of us in the fanbase are excited albeit guarded.

I'm also a big fan of former Ford CEO Alan Mulally, especially with respect to the great work he did at Ford starting in 2006 to turn around that culture and Ford's business. Having "cut my teeth" professionally in the auto industry, I know how political and unhealthy those organizations can be. Ford was in dire need of a new leader and a new direction during the great recession of the early 2000s. Mulally developed a cohesive team, created and communicated a clear and simple strategy, and executed that strategy, which ultimately saved the company. This is a true American success story.

Imagine if Campbell was hired and failed to build a cohesive coaching staff or create clarity for the team about culture, priorities, and strategy. Or if, when Mulally created the One Ford plan, he and his leaders failed to consistently communicate that clear strategy and failed to reinforce that clarity in meetings, when hiring, or when managing a team's performance. How successful would those organizations be? In a word: *not.*

When I came to Hoover Treated Wood Products as a first-time CEO, I was determined to build a healthy, high-performing organization. Having previously had a front-row seat at multiple unhealthy organizations where I was not the CEO, I'd witnessed how confusion and politics result in low morale, low productivity, weak engagement, and predictably subpar business results.

Over my career as a leader, I have come to understand and embrace Patrick Lencioni's four disciplines of organizational health model. Having seen the remarkable results that came from building a cohesive team and creating organizational clarity (disciplines one and two), I set out to build the team and create the necessary clarity that had been lacking previously. And at the risk of sounding arrogant, I executed that well. I formed a great executive team with players from within and outside of the company, and together we created clarity around purpose, values, strategy, and priorities— clarity that had been nonexistent before.

But there are *four* disciplines of organizational health, not *two*. While a team that scores touchdowns on two of every four drives is on a path to the Super Bowl, and a quarterback who completes three out of every four passes over a career will be a lock for the Hall of Fame, anything less than four out of four disciplines mastered results in a less-than-optimal organization.

And there lies my mistake. Being *aware* of discipline three and discipline four (overcommunicating clarity and reinforcing clarity, respectively) and *executing* on them as a leadership team are two different things. My executive team and I realized we would need to practice those last two disciplines with greater passion if we were to succeed in transforming our organization.

Perhaps you have heard that you need to repeat things seven times for people to really understand it. Well, I would argue that seven times is not nearly enough. As a society, we are all so easily distracted these days, me included at times (another of my leadership mistakes), by technology and other demands for our attention, that hearing something seven times barely hits the radar. Repetition dozens, if not hundreds, of times from senior leaders is how employees know what is really important.

Recognizing that we needed to up our game here, my team and I committed to speaking at every possible chance about our company purpose ("to protect people where they live and work") and to giving examples of employees who live our values at every opportunity: Be humble. Get it done right. Serve each other; serve our customers.

And while *communicating* organizational clarity is important, *living* it—reinforcing it through our simple human systems and actions—was an area of opportunity for us as well. Taking that seriously, we immediately increased our focus on reinforcing clarity, by hiring people (and expediting departures) based on our core values, by managing performance based on our key business priorities, by running great meetings focused on the most important things, and by making all key decisions with our company strategy in mind.

Building a healthier organization doesn't happen overnight; cultural muscle memory and historical confusion are not easily overcome. But we have made great strides in building a new, healthier organization by focusing on *all four* disciplines, and the results have been outstanding: Our engagement scores and company retention rates have improved dramatically. Our customer net promoter scores have taken a significant turn in the right direction. And we are winning in the marketplace like never before.

I'm hopeful that my Detroit Lions will be able to say the same this year, and in the years to come.

MISTAKE #2

Failing to Connect

If you can't connect, you can't lead.
—George Bradt and Gillian Davis

FAILING TO CONNECT

Y ears ago, shortly after being promoted into my first true executive position with a technology company, I attended my initial senior leadership team meeting. I was young—full of energy and what I thought were good ideas and opinions. I walked into that meeting ready to make a difference by contributing to the team and solving the important issues facing our company.

It was the CEO's weekly gathering with the leadership team, and he was one of the smartest guys I had ever worked with. He had been a key strategist in defining our market, which ensured we had an early leadership position as the market developed. He had secured investors, hired people who were excited to help this young company achieve its potential, and followed his strategy closely. And while his cup overflowed with smarts and with great strategic approaches and ideas, that cup didn't have any space left in it for other important personal leadership qualities such as openness, transparency, and vulnerability. This leader lacked humility. He was the smartest one in the room—every room—and wanted to make sure everyone knew it.

This meeting began, as was the custom, with a monologue on something the CEO had done particularly well, an award he had won, or an impressive new idea that he had come up with. As he made his opening remarks, though, he said something that wasn't accurate. I knew it and everyone else knew it, but nobody said anything. Being young and a bit naïve, and wanting to make my mark on the team and company, I spoke up to challenge his comment.

"That's not true," I said. "You're mistaken."

As soon as those fateful words hit the air, every head in the room turned in my direction. Clearly, I had shocked the whole lot by challenging our brilliant leader. The entire team braced for the explosion that was about to follow. They had seen this movie before, but no one had given fair warning to their new junior executive peer.

The CEO struck fast. He immediately began dressing me down, belittling me in front of the group, and going on (with some stamina) as to why he was right and I was wrong—why he was smart and I was stupid. And he just kept going. His tirade sent the absolutely clear message to me and the others: *Don't you* dare *ever challenge me in front of this team.* Believe me, it was an error I wasn't about to repeat.

One of my peers, the vice president of marketing, pulled me aside after we walked out of the meeting and said, "We don't *do that* in there."

I thanked him for that obvious insight and shared that it would have been nice to know *before* the meeting.

"If you want to keep your job," the marketing VP continued, "I'd suggest you don't do that again."

(I *did* want to keep that job—I had only been there about a week!)

The message from the CEO that day to me and the others on our team was clear: He was in no way going to show any vulnerability—and we shouldn't either.

The ramifications of his lack of vulnerability went far beyond this one moment of embarrassment for a young, naïve leader, though. It taught every single one of us that we should never show weakness, never ask for help, and stay in our respective lanes. It created a siloed atmosphere in the company at the most senior level that cascaded throughout our business. It created and cemented a culture of advocacy rather than collaboration. When challenges arose across the enterprise, there was no help requested and none was given. Small, solvable problems became bigger, less manageable ones and eventually led to the collapse of the company.

If you were to read the obituary of that company, it would convey that we had strategy problems, product issues, sales troubles, and financial irregularities—all true. But those are all things I *know* we had the smarts to solve early on, had our leadership team shared them and worked through them together. The lack of vulnerability demonstrated by the leader, the ensuing lack of relationships and teamwork on the executive team, and therefore the lack of help we gave one another ensured that our small problems would grow into unmanageable ones. Relatively quickly, our young company, which initially showed such great promise, imploded.

This lack of vulnerability and humility is one way leaders can fail to connect to the people they lead, and I've seen, multiple times, the negative consequences of those mistakes.

What follows are seven examples of the "failure to connect" mistake, along with recommendations from seven great (and vulnerable!) leaders who were willing to share them.

LACKING VULNERABILITY

Dr. William Morice II, CEO, Mayo Clinic Laboratories

Physicians are not known for their vulnerability. As a senior leader in one of the most respected healthcare research organizations in the world, I should probably cite some study that supports this statement, but I think vulnerability is a tough thing to measure. However, my own qualitative research—first in looking at myself in the mirror, and also in talking to peers and colleagues during my 30 years as a leader, researcher, and practitioner—supports that statement.

While I can't cite published research, I *can* share an expert opinion relevant to this story and the organization I lead—an opinion shared with me by Dr. Richard Boyatzis, an expert in organizational emotional intelligence who has worked extensively with academic medical centers. Of the medical professions Dr. Boyatzis has worked with, he has found that pathologists, surgeons, and radiologists are the three groups most resistant to change, likely due to their high reliance on data-driven cognitive pathways. As the leader previously responsible for the department of pathology, and now as CEO of Mayo Clinic Laboratories, a fast-paced, ever-changing business enterprise, I find that this presents a real challenge. I suspect the reason for this general lack of vulnerability within these physician specialties is that these professionals confuse vulnerability with competence. The risks of incompetence are often high for these doctors, sometimes meaning the difference between life and death.

Can you be a good leader who is both vulnerable *and* competent? I've learned over the course of my career as a leader that vulnerability is a key trait in leadership excellence. In the work my senior leadership team did with The Table Group, not only did we learn about vulnerability-based trust, but we put into practice what we learned. The outcome during our work together—at our first off-site session and since then—has been better, more open conversations; greater debate; and ultimately, better decisions for our organization. Although it may sound touchy-feely (and I always worry that my academic colleagues will think that), on the contrary it is anything but. This trait of vulnerability, which I try to model for my senior leaders and encourage across our departments, has led to improved business outcomes; increased employee engagement; and most important, better patient care—the primary reason the Mayo Clinic exists.

But *saying* we are going to be vulnerable and actually *doing* so are still challenges. I am far from perfect at this. In fact, my ability to demonstrate vulnerability in the midst of change was put to the test recently during a business change initiative I hoped to implement.

For weeks I worked on a presentation about this new initiative in hopes of getting buy-in from the senior executive team I report to. The meeting went well, and the executives offered their support. I was thrilled with the decision and excited about the prospect of sharing this news with my team. I expected they would be supportive and ready to jump in to make it happen.

But that's not how they responded.

Few of my leaders and their teams knew much about the initiative. I hadn't briefed them in detail, and I hadn't asked for their opinions or advice. Rather, I had inadvertently excluded them from the process. So, while I was thrilled that the initiative was supported by the executives, I realized it meant little if my team hadn't bought in and committed to the initiative's success. In my excitement, I had skipped this important step. I had made a leadership error and needed to find a way to recover. Though I could have denied the mistake, forced the issue, and demanded support, this was not the kind of leader I wanted to be. After all, hadn't we agreed to be vulnerable and honest with one another?

I immediately began setting up meetings across the department's divisions to admit my mistake, make a proper and thorough case for the new initiative, and ask for their help, buy-in, and support.

Although it was an example of "better late than never," it appears my team appreciated my honesty and vulnerability. The approach and apology addressed their concerns and lessened their resistance to the forthcoming change. They gave me their support, and we are now aligned around the new initiative, which is key to the future success of the business. Leading indicators as the change initiative is implemented point to a more successful long-term business based on these changes.

My hope is that this vulnerability-based approach to leadership will be a legacy I leave at the Mayo Clinic and with the people I have led during my career.

FAILING TO GET TO KNOW YOUR TEAM PERSONALLY

Chris Cohen, Director, Large Enterprise Sales, LinkedIn

I played basketball at Seattle Pacific University for a coach named Jeff Hironaka. He was not only the best coach I have ever had, but also one of the best leaders I have ever known. From an X's and O's perspective, he knew the game as well as anyone and was a great practice and game manager, but that is not what set him apart from other coaches. His real gift as a coach and leader was the authentic care he showed for his players. Coach Hironaka got to know us personally, took great interest in our development as players and as people, and always put the team goals and his players' goals ahead of his own. As a direct result of this approach, we worked harder and achieved greater success as a team, as student athletes, and eventually as business professionals than we would have otherwise. I learned more about leadership from him than practically any other person in my life.

So you'd think that when I took on my first leadership position for Gallo Wine Company, I would have immediately followed his lead. But I didn't.

Upon taking the position as a district manager, I immediately got out in the field to survey accounts and begin assessing how well individuals on the team were doing, all in preparation for my first team meeting. In one of my first store visits, two of my team members were in the store at the time, building a large wine display in the front lobby. I walked in and said a quick hello to my two new reps and then jumped right into business: pulling out my clipboard, making my way around the store, and filling out our standard survey form. I failed to spend even two minutes connecting with these two direct reports or to pause and think this would be a good time to build rapport. Even worse, I didn't ask if they needed help building their display. I was much more focused on how I was establishing myself in my new position and having these reps see my new level of importance. Through their lens, I have no doubt, they were thinking I was nothing more than a six-foot-seven-inch jackass.

It didn't take me long in that position to realize that my approach was a poor one. First impressions are important in any relationship, especially as a new leader. Although I worked to repair the relationships soon after, a lot of damage was done. It took me a while to recover from that initial error.

This early mistake has been a constant point of reflection for me as I have taken on new, progressively larger leadership roles, first within the consumer packaged goods industry and then in the SaaS tech industry. Now, when I take on a new role with a new team or onboard a new team member, channeling Coach Hironaka's approach in getting to know his team members and building foundational relationships is the first thing I work toward. I want to know each team member as a whole person, not just their professional side. What excites them about life? What motivates them and gets them up in the morning? What weighs on them and holds them back from becoming their best selves? My ultimate question early on with a new team member is: *How can I add value to this individual and serve them as their new leader?* I keep this question at the forefront of my mind throughout my time working with that specific member of our team.

As I moved past that initial experience of being the proverbial "bull in a china shop" leader, I have recognized increasingly over time the importance of quieting your ego and not overtrying to prove your importance to your team. It eventually dawned on me that when I chose to behave this way, I was not proving myself to the people I was trying to impress in the first place, but rather working to prove myself to *me*. Rechanneling that effort and energy externally to deeply understand those I have the opportunity to serve as a leader has been much more rewarding and fruitful.

As an example, five years ago when I became the new vice president of sales, I took over a senior sales team of people who were both older than me and had been in the industry much longer than me. Moving from being a former peer to their leader, it could have been easy to fall back into the trap of working to impress versus serve. Luckily, I had the earlier teaching moment to draw upon so I would not make that same mistake.

This "team member first" approach was reinforced for me recently when I had the opportunity to connect with one of my former direct reports. We sat down together and caught up, and she articulated how much my personal approach to leadership meant to her. During our conversation, she recalled a specific time period that was incredibly trying for her and expressed significant gratitude for our relationship and my supportive approach as her leader. I was honored by her words and fulfilled because she felt led and cared for as a person versus an employee.

Caring about the people you lead isn't something that can be faked. During my playing days, Coach Hironaka showed genuine care with small, simple acts that showed all of his players what they meant to him. In fact, he never stopped with these simple acts. Each year on my birthday, Thanksgiving, and Christmas, I still receive a personal text message or phone call from him, wishing me and my family well. He still does this for all his former players—that's hundreds of players over a 30-plus-year coaching career. My hope and objective are that my effort, in serving those I have the opportunity to lead, has an impact on them that resembles the impact Coach Hironaka's approach had on me.

HAVING TOO MANY MEMBERS ON THE EXECUTIVE TEAM
James Blackledge, CEO, Mutual of Omaha

At Mutual of Omaha, we are extremely proud of our relationship with the iconic television show *Wild Kingdom*. But as chairman and CEO, I want to make sure I am *affiliated* with a wild kingdom, not *leading* one.

I am an actuary by trade. Actuarial science is the discipline that applies mathematical and statistical methods to assess risk in insurance, pension, finance, investment, and other industries and professions. Actuaries are professionals who apply rigorous mathematics in order to model matters of uncertainty in helping companies assess and manage risk.

I started my career at Mutual of Omaha as an actuary and have held multiple positions that deal directly with risk. Those include leadership positions in our group and individual business units as well as senior executive roles as chief risk officer and chief information officer. In each of those roles, advising the business about risk and taking calculated risks was something I took seriously, and also something I enjoyed. As CEO, I have continued to take calculated risks with big business decisions, including the sale of Mutual of Omaha Bank and, more recently, the decision to invest in a new corporate campus.

When I took over as CEO in 2015, I built my leadership team with risk in mind. For business reasons, to be more inclusive and to increase diversity of experience and opinion, I grew my executive team to 17 senior leaders. Adding more people to the team, thereby increasing diversity of opinion, would help *decrease* risk, right?

Wrong.

As the size of the team increased, the vulnerability, willingness to take on tough conversations, and willingness to hold one another accountable decreased. Decisions took longer to make, and meetings became longer, less productive, and more difficult to manage. Clarity for the team—and therefore, for the organization—declined. Increasing the size of the team actually *increased* risk—the very thing I was trying to decrease.

Although my intentions were pure, another science came into play here: physics. In addition to the scheduling headaches associated with aligning 17 senior leaders' calendars, I have come to realize it is physically impossible to have difficult, important conversations on a consistent basis with a group of that size. And one of the key responsibilities of a senior leadership team is to have those difficult but important conversations. Recognizing the mistake, I pared my team down to a much more manageable nine senior leaders, and more recently pared it again to eight. As a result, the vulnerability has increased, the tough issues are brought up more readily, the decisions are faster and better, and our organizational clarity has increased. Nowhere is that more apparent than in our daily meetings, each of which is designed to focus our conversations on the most important things.

Every business is different, and I don't believe "one size fits all" when it comes to an executive team. But if your team is too big to tackle the most important and difficult issues, or too big to meet regularly for those critical discussions that result in better decisions, you're likely taking on unnecessary risk.

FAILING TO LISTEN

Joe Terry, CEO, Culture Partners

It was a beautiful day on the Big Island—hot, but that's expected. Relatively still water and a mild breeze were not expected, but a nice and welcome surprise. These were great conditions for a personal record (PR) in the Ironman World Championships in Kona, Hawaii.

Due in part to the great conditions and some extra focus in my training, the swim went well, and after the transition, I was in a good place. Fifty miles into the 112-mile bike leg, and I was feeling really good. My inclination was to push harder—"pedal to the metal," as they say. *Maybe, just maybe*, I began to think, *I might not only beat my personal best but blow it away.*

But soon I heard my coach's words in my ear: *Slow down and eat.*

I fought those words, thinking, *I am feeling so good, and I'm really not that hungry.* I was inclined not to follow his guidance.

But I heard his voice again, this time with greater intensity: *Slow down.*

I knew he was right. There was still a long way to go and many great obstacles ahead, namely the headwinds of the Queen K Highway and a marathon in the blistering hot sun of Kona. If I didn't slow down, conserve my energy, and get the fuel I needed, this would get ugly. This was not a sprint but quite literally (more than) a marathon. Although my gut told me otherwise, I acquiesced.

It turned out to be the right decision. By slowing down, I made sure I had the energy necessary to get through the headwind on the back half of the bike ride and the strength I needed to endure the intense heat during the 26.2-mile run. I didn't crash and burn, and once the long day was over, I did get that Kona PR I was seeking.

I wish I could say I always slow down when I need to and listen as well as I should, but I don't.

Both in racing and in my roles leading organizations, I like to go fast. I have a lot of confidence in my gut decisions; the little voice in my mind always tells me, *Trust your gut. Make decisions fast. Don't waste time.* But that's not always the right choice.

In fact, slowing down and listening to the people on my team and across the organization has almost always led to better decisions. My people are close to the action—sometimes closer to the business and to our customers than I am—and therefore they see things I don't. I've learned over time that people need to *weigh in* before they *buy in*. Seeking first to understand, as the renowned businessman Stephen Covey points out, is important, especially when talking about the most important things and the biggest decisions in your organization.

When I've resisted my tendency to make decisions alone in order to go fast, I have found that our company has benefited. When our leaders are involved in the decision-making process, not only are decisions better, but the business is stronger—because including my team ensures that they feel appreciated and respected, which leads to greater commitment on their part.

Distancing yourself from the competition in an individual sport is good, but distancing yourself from the people in your organization is not so good for organizations that are trying to win—and win *together*.

BEING TOO INVOLVED

G. Shawn Hunter, President and Founder, Mindscaling, author of *Small Acts of Leadership*

It was 2006. Mariah Carey and Beyoncé topped the charts, the movie *Borat* was released, Google purchased YouTube for $1.6 billion, Pluto's planet status was revoked, Nintendo released the Wii, and Italy won the World Cup.

At this same moment in time, our mighty little company Targeted Learning was gaining speed and momentum. We were creating on-demand and live video learning content. Somehow, miraculously, we were ahead of the market. Just a few years earlier we were defining the market, and now competition was rising swiftly and steadily. I remember at one company off-site retreat, we had identified a handful of companies entering our space. The following year we lost count.

We were big enough to have people dedicated to sales, marketing, operations, technology, service, partnerships, and more. Yet we were also small enough that the 20 of us could still keep in close touch. And during this time, I had my hands in everything.

I was working with our technology team to design and build our next-generation user experience, creating the content and product we sold, and leading or participating in almost all the sales initiatives. I remember at one point we had a fabulous sales guy who created a chart depicting who worked on what in the company—kind of like a Venn diagram showing everyone's role. My name was everywhere. I felt personally responsible for everything.

And I was stressed. I didn't realize or understand how stressed I was until we sold the company in early 2007, and I collapsed for a few months in an exhausted fog. The problem—my mistake—was that I was having a hard time letting go. I was having a hard time placing trust in my colleagues.

What I have come to believe now is that I couldn't let go of a personal sense of ownership and responsibility. I felt I had to add my comments or approval to every strategy, every project, and every decision. Upon reflection, I can see now that I was lacking appropriate humility and overvaluing my importance to our work. I wasn't trusting the contributions of others, and the fundamental cause was that I didn't yet possess a strong sense of gratitude for their work. After all, if I have my hands in everything and I'm the principal reason for the success, why develop a sense of gratitude for someone else's contribution?

Once we sold the company to Skillsoft, entering the much larger corporation as a small division and product line, it was no longer possible for me to contribute everywhere—although initially, I did try. I would ask to sit in on contract meetings, intellectual property discussions, and marketing copy reviews. After a while, it was clear I was diluting my efforts, and I wasn't making meaningful contributions.

For me, the key was to learn and practice a deepened sense of gratitude for others, which in turn allowed me to give trust and let go. Targeted Learning was handicapped by my insistence to participate in (maybe even control) everything, but once we entered the much bigger world of Skillsoft, it became impossible. That's when I learned to be grateful for my colleagues and their skills and contributions.

As I traveled the world working with team members within Skillsoft, I began to actively let each collaborator know how grateful I was—grateful for the invitation to be helpful, grateful for learning from them, grateful for the opportunity to work with their clients. Eventually, this practiced and learned sense of gratitude allowed me to let go of what I could not control and instead focus on my real expertise.

The need to be overly involved in every aspect of the organization disappeared. I felt relief at the reduced pressure from what I couldn't (and didn't need to) control, and the people in my organization felt more empowered, respected, and appreciated for their great contributions.

I have an expression I use in my writing: *Only do what only you can do.* By following this guidance, I know my work is more valuable to others, and my impact as a leader is deeper and stronger.

FAILING TO EXPRESS GRATITUDE

Dave Kroll, Vice President Communications, Automation Anywhere

Sunday, July 10, 1994, was a beautiful, sunny day for baseball at Candlestick Park in San Francisco. With rumors of a baseball strike in the weeks ahead, fans showed up in droves to watch the San Francisco Giants play the Philadelphia Phillies in the last game before the all-star break. Although the fans came to watch their team, they also got to witness the "breakout" performance of a South Bay musical acoustic duo: the not-so-cleverly named Dave and Mike. I was the Dave.

Despite our not-so-massive following in the South Bay area of San Francisco, we had submitted our demo tape to the Giants the year prior, and with luck, a cancellation came with short notice just days before that baseball game. The call went out to Dave and Mike to sing the national anthem.

Anxious and exhilarated, we sang our two-part harmony version of the anthem for the largest crowd we had ever found (or would ever find) ourselves performing in front of—and as we wrapped up, all 48,263 fans gave us a standing ovation. For the rest of the ballgame, fans gave us shout-outs or high-fives when they saw us in the stands. I understood their recognition was more for the song than for us, but it still felt pretty darn good. Applause, along with tips in the tip jar when we played our three-hour sets at much smaller venues, was the only form of gratitude Mike and I typically received for our music. These simple gestures by our audiences were always much appreciated and inspired us to play and sing our hearts out.

When I started working in technology firms in Silicon Valley, the gratitude was much harder to come by. In the analytical, fast-paced world of high tech, critiques of my work were much more plentiful than the *attaboys*. As a young professional in the communications industry, I remember the draft of my first press release marked up with what felt like dozens upon dozens of mistakes and corrections highlighted in a bright red marker, affectionately left on my desk chair by my supervisor.

Nice.

I remember another time when I sent a company-wide email to about 30 people and shortly thereafter received a reply-all back from our CEO, with redline edits and grammar corrections as an example for all of us to learn from.

Ouch.

Both instances were painful and embarrassing, especially since my mom is a retired English teacher. (Sorry, Jane!) But these were not exceptions at work. In the office, I'd often go weeks at a time between compliments, whereas rarely a day went by without comments or criticisms by my supervisors—intended to improve my performance, of course.

When I was promoted into my first management job, I followed the example I had been taught by my previous leaders. I thought my job was to make my employees better by focusing on correcting their flaws and mistakes in order to improve *their* performance. So, I seldom gave praise and instead gave critical and negative feedback on a regular basis, like a parent focusing on the one B+ rather than the six A's on a report card. My people felt underappreciated and at times, I'm sure, demoralized.

This was a costly error I made as a young leader, and it contributed to some truly great people leaving my team and my company for other opportunities. The loss of those key people—at least in part due to my mistakes—really stung. It was something that stayed with me and shook me up a bit, motivating me to look for better ways to improve my leadership abilities.

I read books about leadership and sought advice from leaders I respected. Addressing my mistakes head-on, I tried experimenting with different forms of recognition and more frequent "on-the-spot" compliments to acknowledge good work. It's amazing how a "thank you" helps people feel appreciated.

I arranged more team dinners after big projects that had required extra-long hours and sacrifice by the team. For several teams, I printed up matching dog tags to improve team cohesion as we went through challenges together, and I gave out medals for standout performances.

Other actions included awarding small cash bonuses for great efforts or delivering a bottle of wine to a teammate for doing something *right*. I think the team appreciated the authentic effort and intent behind it, and the size of the gift or bonus didn't really matter. On occasion, I even got "the Mike" to help me sing "Happy Birthday" in two-part harmony over the phone to employees on their special day. Some of these things were a bit unorthodox, but they achieved the goal of showing appreciation and recognizing employees—something I had not done naturally.

What I learned was that in life and work, people appreciate the small things. And I realized an important insight: Recognition is free! It's been well researched that people don't stay at a job for the money; they stay because of their boss, their team, an inspiring mission, and the strong company culture. Many leaders are *way* too stingy, thinking that if they recognize or reward too many people, it will water down and reduce the value of that recognition. I've never been a part of a company or heard of one, ever, where people left because leadership recognized people too much. Try it and see what happens with your teams.

While a number of companies *talk* about engagement and valuing their employees, I joined Rackspace Technology in 2013 and knew I'd found a company that actually *lived* it. Graham Weston, the cofounder and former Rackspace CEO and chairman, said this about work in a 2010 TEDx Talk: "What we all want is to be valued members of a winning team on an inspiring mission."

Read that again. Isn't that true for most everyone?

These were not just words. They were lived every day and reinforced in the actions by "Rackers" up, down, and across the organization. It's a unifying statement that guided employees on how to treat each other—not just as teammates, but as human beings. It permeated processes like new employee orientation and how leaders managed their employees. It also helped create an environment I liked to call the "no a-hole factor," where inspiring leaders could flourish, and where self-focused, egotistical, or harsh leaders would eventually leave the company due to "organ rejection."

There are so many other ways to make people feel valued, such as by stepping out of their way, focusing on their strengths, allowing their great ideas to flourish, and being open and authentic with them. Leaders who demonstrate these behaviors can create a cohesive, motivated, and engaged team.

In the end, for me, leadership is about aligning people's gifts and strengths with where the company is going and where their strengths are needed most. Focusing on people's strengths brings their passion alive in the workplace. And regular and authentic recognition is one of the cheapest and easiest ways not only to keep people motivated and inspired, but also to pull their best work and effort from them.

People are smart. I've learned so much more from the people I managed than I ever taught them. In many ways, learning to express gratitude was a key part of my growth as a leader. Today, as the vice president of communications at Automation Anywhere, I carry with me the same enthusiasm for appreciation and gratitude, and see these small acts of leadership helping me to navigate the day-to-day challenges of a high-tech business.

LACKING HUMILITY

Vibhu Sharma, Executive Vice President and CFO, Pacific Life

Growing up, I wanted to change my name to Mike. Not to "be like Mike" as per the popular Nike campaign from that era, but actually to *become* a Mike.

As a new kid in my grade school, and in the country for that matter, I already looked different and spoke differently, and I didn't want the additional attention that an unusual name like Vibhu would bring. It's embarrassing to say now that I was embarrassed by it.

As I acclimated to my new school, city, and country, and started to do well in school, however, my self-confidence began to grow. And my natural personality—a big, fun-loving personality—began to show itself.

The years progressed, and I earned my degree from Southern Methodist University, achieved my CPA designation, achieved partner at KPMG, and was promoted into a series of greater executive responsibilities at Zurich Insurance Group. With each success, my confidence continued to grow. The problem is that it grew too much. I began to regularly cross the line from appropriate confidence to arrogance, and therein lies the mistake I want to share.

I was alerted to this issue with some honest, direct feedback given to me by the Zurich CEO as I was being promoted to the role of business unit CEO and UK country head. He said that great employees and great leaders are both smart and humble, and that I would need to "lean in" to that second quality if I were going to reach my potential as a person and as a leader.

Smart and humble. I liked that. And as humbling as it was to hear from my leader that I needed to show greater humility, I knew he was right.

C. S. Lewis famously wrote that "true humility is not thinking less of yourself, it's thinking of yourself less." I needed to be better at putting others first and the company first, and not thinking about myself quite so much.

In an effort to up my humility game, I have "leaned in" to three things:

1. *Getting to know the members of the team I lead personally and putting their needs first.* Those who know me know how passionate I am about my family. As much as I love and am dedicated to my work, my faith and my family come first. And as a leader, I've come to realize that long after the quarterly results are forgotten, employees will remember the leaders who took an interest in them personally; invested in their development; and knew their passions, hopes, dreams, and families. Raising money for a team member running a marathon and acknowledging her success publicly . . . buying wine for a corporate function from the home region in Italy where a team member's family originated . . . orchestrating a practical joke on an unsuspecting team member based on their passions or personality . . . pausing to ask about an employee's family prior to diving deep into the numbers in a one-on-one—these are examples of ways I've tried to be more humble and put others first. I also love that these acknowledgments reveal to my team the fun side of

my personality. This approach serves as a great way to continue to develop the culture that we are so passionate about at Pacific Life (PL).

2. *Putting the company first over my function.* I've become a big believer in team over self, and especially in The Table Group concept that if an organization is going to be successful, each leader needs to believe and act as though the team they are *on* is more important than the team they *lead*. Rather than take pride in and advocate for the team *I* lead first— the Finance Senior Leadership Team (SLT)—I know that my priority must be the Pacific Life Management Committee. And as we work hard to create a One PL culture, every leader must humbly embrace this concept if we are to achieve our desired results.

3. *Being vulnerable by admitting when I've made a mistake.* I recently attended a board meeting and (in a moment I now regret) spoke out of turn, interrupting a peer. Doing so made *me* the focus in front of the board and not the peer, whom I admire a great deal. I knew immediately I shouldn't have done it, and I apologized to that peer as soon as the meeting was over. Importantly, I also went to the team I lead in our next SLT meeting and told them what I'd done, how it had been a big mistake, and what I had learned from the incident. Vulnerability is a key component of humility and is a characteristic of all the best leaders I have ever known. And the more senior you are in an organization, the

more important it becomes, because people watch and then emulate senior leaders. Humility and vulnerability cascade down organizations, just as arrogance and pride do.

Having made efforts with these approaches and others, I am now proud to say that I am perfect at being humble. Just kidding. I have a long way to go, and the members of both the team I am on and the team I lead will tell you that. But if I continue to lean in to humility by putting others and the company above myself, allow my true personality to guide me, and readily admit my mistakes, it will have a huge impact on me, my teams, and our entire organization.

MISTAKE #3

Running Truly
Awful Meetings

*A meeting is an event at which the
minutes are kept and the hours are lost.*

—attributed to Joseph Stillwell

RUNNING TRULY AWFUL MEETINGS

——

Years ago, I was hired as the vice president of Western US and Canada for a technology company headquartered on the East Coast of the United States. I flew back to the company headquarters for my first executive team meeting, excited about meeting my new colleagues and working together with my new peers on the most important things facing our company.

In the first few hours of this two-day executive meeting, the team covered the following issues:

- Key accounts

- Customer support issues and churn

- Business unit status reports

- The right coffee for the breakroom

- Employee performance issues

- Implementing Sarbanes–Oxley compliance regulations

- Repaving the headquarters parking lot

- New HR benefits options

- A new product version release
- The new employee smartphone policy
- A potential acquisition
- A potential future meeting
  (making this a meeting *about* meetings!)

It was a smorgasbord of topics: some administrative, some strategic, some tactical, some important to the business and this executive team, and many (probably most) clearly not worthy of our time.

On the cover of Patrick Lencioni's book *Death by Meeting*, there is a picture of an employee at the end of the conference table with his head down, either asleep or bored to tears. Not only does the title say a lot about deadly meetings, but the picture adds salt to the wound. And everyone in my executive meeting that day—at least everyone who was not presenting at the moment—felt like that cover guy.

As leaders, if we are honest with ourselves, we've all probably led that very meeting at some point over the course of our careers. In the book, Patrick presents a very specific meeting model that has been vetted with thousands of executive teams over the years. He makes the case that there should be different types of meetings for different specific purposes, and that by mixing up the purposes and inserting random topics for each meeting, you end up with "meeting stew," which never tastes good.

In this executive team meeting, the various chefs were making the biggest pot of this stew I'd ever tasted, and every bite was predictably hard to swallow. Eyes glazed over and unanimous boredom set in as leaders took turns presenting slide after slide after slide.

The agenda meandered aimlessly from item to item without closure to any of the items discussed, and I honestly began to question my decision to take this position and join this company.

As my mind wandered, a peer sitting next to me—my sales leadership counterpart with responsibility for the Eastern US—gave me a look that said he wanted my attention. He was taking out a piece of scratch paper and looking at me as if to say, *This note is for you.*

I became interested and silently guessed at what the note might say. Maybe he was writing out a short "Welcome to the company!" and offering support as I worked to become acclimated. Or perhaps there was an account with a presence in both of our geographies that he wanted to strategize on and work on together. Knowing that he previously had worked with many people across the company, I thought maybe he was sharing insight on some of the leaders or employees present to help me as I established myself with my team. I highly anticipated his note, whatever it said, because I knew it had to be more interesting than the multiple random topics and blather that were this meeting.

But when he handed the short note to me, I opened it to find only three words *Kill, Me,* and *Now*:

Kill Me Now!

I knew instantly that this leader was going to be a great friend of mine in the company, because that's exactly what I was thinking: *Kill me now!* But the reality was that everyone in the room was thinking the same thing. There was absolutely no clarity as to the purpose of the meeting or what we were trying to accomplish. And in the instances where we did make some progress on a topic or decision, there was neither confirmation of that decision nor of the team's commitment to that decision. At no time during that meeting did we end a conversation with clarity about what was decided and what we would communicate.

A leader whom I respect serves as the chief of staff for the communications group in a large technology company. He is extremely passionate about good meetings, having learned something from a Japanese saying that he applies to his business—loosely translated, *No target, no meeting.* In other words, if there is no clarity about the meeting's purpose, the meeting doesn't happen.

But meetings play an important role in organizations. As the "game time" of business, they can be a strategic tool and lead to competitive advantage—*if* they are managed correctly. Good meetings lead to good decisions, and bad meetings lead to bad decisions. There are no two ways about it. The key is to make sure meetings are structured appropriately to achieve the desired outcomes, focus on the most important things, start and end with clarity, and don't waste valuable time.

In the pages that follow, seven great leaders not only share their mistakes related to meetings, but offer their advice on how to avoid those mistakes to improve your business.

ALLOWING CONFUSION ABOUT MEETINGS

Linda Copple Trout, Chief Justice, Idaho Supreme Court (retired)

I served on the Idaho Supreme Court as a justice for 15 years—seven as chief justice and eight as an associate justice on the high court. In that time, I sat on over 1,800 cases; of those cases, I authored more than 400.

In a court of law, there is great clarity about a number of things, starting with clarity about who is leading the case: the judge. It's clear what will be discussed and decided in each case, and specific rules and known, acceptable behaviors are followed to make sure order is kept and ensure justice is served. Protocols allow for appropriate debate, and procedures are followed as decisions are being made. And once decisions are made, there is not only understanding about what those decisions are but documentation of those decisions to ensure further clarity. The inner workings of the courtroom are clear to everyone involved.

When I left the bench and took over as administrative director of the courts, though, I learned quickly that clarity was far less prevalent in other areas of the organization—especially in meetings. Often, our meetings lacked clarity of purpose, were uneven in participation, and had no clear process. Decisions were often unrecorded or not communicated. And my sense, having talked to business and community leaders, was that this problem was pervasive across many organizations outside of the courts and other government entities.

Not only did I recognize this trend across the organization, but it also became obvious that my own executive leadership team staff meetings—for which I was responsible—also lacked clarity. And that's a big mistake.

In any organization, employees watch the executive team very closely. That goes for all behaviors, including how meetings are run. If the leadership team runs poor meetings, that problem cascades down and perpetuates itself.

After recognizing the organization's challenge—the uncertainty the Idaho Courts faced around their meetings—I took steps to correct the problem. I talked to the courts' chief information officer, who introduced me to a consultant who had helped align his team. The consultant then acquainted our team with a good, proven process for running effective, productive meetings.

After some work together, the Idaho Courts' leadership team and I agreed on a new approach to our meetings: First, we would determine appropriate behaviors for the meeting. Second, the meeting leader would ensure we started and ended with clarity. Our goal was to be clear up front about why we were there, and clear when we finished as to what had been decided, what the next steps were, and how we would communicate. With discipline in applying the process, our meetings became more productive, our leadership team became better aligned, and we set the tone for meetings across the organization.

Because I was both the first female associate justice and later the first female chief justice, early on in those roles I was worried about making mistakes lest they cause problems for future generations of women seeking a similar seat. But worse than making mistakes would be to learn nothing from them. Fortunately, that did not happen here. Taking quick, decisive action after appropriate consideration—including changing poorly run meetings to those that were productive and clear—worked for the Idaho Courts and worked elsewhere across the organization.

RUNNING MEETINGS WITHOUT PURPOSE

Roy Aggarwal, President, RAGGSTR Enterprises

What's the mission?

As a pilot, I always ask myself that question first when I have the opportunity to fly, and the same is true of my pilot peers. Performing a medical evacuation, delivering a foster puppy to its new home, flying a group of executives on a business trip or a golfing excursion (all actual missions I have completed in the past year)—each requires different planning and preparation if the mission is to be successful.

As Yogi Berra once said, "If you don't know where you are going, you'll end up someplace else." Funny, and also true. But for a pilot, if the mission isn't clear and the flight plan isn't well thought out, the effort is not only unlikely to succeed, but likely to be dangerous and irresponsible.

In addition to being a pilot, I am an entrepreneur who owns and operates a restaurant that serves, in my opinion, the best pizza in Boise, Idaho. And if that seems like a strange combination of professions, you should see the rest of my resume: chief of staff in a Fortune 500 corporation, procurement officer, warehouse worker, international supply-chain director, Uber driver, flight instructor, chef, director of project management. Pretty random assortment of roles, right? I do like trying new things and learning new skills. Variety is what I consider the spice of life.

In every role along the way, though, there has been one constant: truly awful meetings. And as the leader in some of these situations, I was the one most responsible for that mistake. Having led some lousy meetings, though, and suffered through many more, I've become a passionate proponent of truly *great* meetings, and I have a few recommendations for other leaders.

- *Start with clarity.* I started my story with the question *What's the mission?*—and the answer to that question is the very way I now like to start every meeting. What are we trying to accomplish in this meeting, and what outcomes are we expecting? Is it a check-in/update meeting? A tactical meeting to check on progress against goals? A strategic meeting to dive deep into an important topic? A good flight plan is planned out with desired outcomes, and my experience indicates that meetings in organizations should start with the same clarity.

- *Use a real-time agenda.* When flying, the weather can change so quickly that you don't finalize a flight plan until immediately before the flight. It would be crazy to build a flight plan on last week's forecast! Similarly, things change so quickly in business and in organizations that setting an agenda a week before—or even the day before—often is not ideal. A good meeting requires talking about the most important things, and a real-time agenda will ensure that.

- *Agree on virtual meeting rules.* In the flying world, visual flight rules (VFRs) are a set of regulations that govern the conditions required to operate aircraft with visual reference to the ground and horizon. Having witnessed and led a number of lousy virtual meetings, I'm a big advocate for virtual meeting rules (VMRs). These are simple agreements and clear expectations for making the most out of a great technology advancement like Zoom or Microsoft Teams—platforms that offer great advantages from an efficiency standpoint, but also a lot of opportunity for distraction and suboptimal outcomes.

I have learned that when it comes to the five behaviors required of great teams (as set out by Patrick Lencioni in his book *The Five Dysfunctions of a Team*), it is far more difficult to achieve success in these behaviors when the meeting is virtual. In a virtual context, the leader needs to be especially deliberate about practicing vulnerability, mining for conflict, forcing clarity around decisions and actions, and demonstrating a willingness to give and receive feedback—all of which are necessary for the team to get the most out of virtual meetings and achieve collective results.

One rule related to visuals is agreeing to keep cameras on. If a team is talking about important things, body language and facial expressions are a big part of understanding one another. It also keeps everyone else from wondering if "cameras off" attendees are multitasking, sleeping, or clipping their toenails (yuck!)—all activities that are not conducive to getting the most out of meeting time together as a team.

- *End with clarity.* A consultant friend coached me and my previous executive team to always save five minutes at the end of the meeting to align on decisions and actions, what *will* be communicated consistently after the meeting, and (importantly) what *will not* be communicated after the meeting. In my pilot's world, we call this a "mission debrief," and it is a golden opportunity to go over what went well, what could be done to improve, and whatever feedback needs to be given to (or gotten from) the crew. My experience is that the final five minutes of a meeting is often when attendees get distracted; they start thinking about whatever meeting they have next rather than aligning on what was agreed upon and what will be communicated after their current meeting. And a lack of alignment on decisions and communication, especially by a senior leadership team, can result in confusion, politics, and wasted efforts downstream in an organization.

Thank you for being my copilot on this short trip. The mission was to give leaders some things to consider and apply to make their meetings more effective and their businesses more successful. I hope that that mission has been accomplished.

HOLDING ONLY ONE MEETING

Ali Rabe, Idaho State Senator and Executive Director, Jesse Tree

A lawyer, a politician, and a philanthropist walk into a bar. Stop me if you have heard this one . . .

I don't really have a punch line to finish with here, other than the fact that I am all three of those things. It's an unusual professional combination, I'll admit, but I am grateful for both my legal training and the jobs that allow me to serve the good people in my hometown of Boise and the great state of Idaho.

The first two roles don't require further introduction, but the third does. I am the executive director of Jesse Tree, a nonprofit whose purpose is to help people in our community stay in their homes—to proactively keep people off the streets. And it is in this role that I made the mistake I want to share.

Soon after I took on the executive director role at Jesse Tree, the organization started to experience tremendous growth. We secured more gifts and grants that led to larger budgets, additional staff, and most important, more capacity to keep a growing population of home-insecure people in their homes. To increase communication for the growing organization, I implemented a daily all-hands meeting—our *only* meeting—with the intention of discussing the most important issues and ensuring alignment for the team. Although well intended, those daily huddles quickly became firefighting sessions as we reacted to the urgent issues, but not always the important ones.

I had implemented a process that was not achieving its desired outcomes and was preventing us from addressing critical issues.

The mistake here was trying to tackle all things, both important and urgent, in a singular daily meeting. In law school, with the help of Richard Michael Fischl and Jeremy Paul's book *Getting to Maybe*, my fellow law students and I became fluent in finding ways to see all sides of an issue; as lawyers, this would be critical were we to present a case to a judge or jury. We also learned how to ask meaningful questions that enabled us to be proactive—not reactive—in our work. But at Jesse Tree, we had become reactive rather than proactive, violating both my own training and our company's strategic approach to the homelessness issue.

Recognizing the mistake, my leadership team and I implemented a new process for our meetings. This time, we created separate meetings to address those things that were urgent and those that were important. Aligned to Patrick Lencioni's book *Death by Meeting*, we now have daily standups once weekly for administrative, cultural, and alignment purposes; weekly tactical meetings to move the business forward and to check in on our progress against our key objectives; strategic meetings to give the big issues the time they deserve; and quarterly off-sites to develop the important relationships on the team and to establish where the organization is headed.

I have come to believe that this new meeting cadence and structure have enabled us to proactively make better decisions; helped us become a healthier, more successful organization; and enabled us to have a greater impact on our community.

Need evidence?

In lawyer speak, consider Exhibit A: In the year after implementing our new meeting model, we were able to help prevent more than 1,100 families from being evicted—doubling that figure from the previous year. For Exhibit B, consider our strategic meetings related to fundraising. Because of careful, thoughtful planning of the organization's annual giving event and auction this year, we raised over $300,000, more than doubling the funds raised from the previous year's event.

I'm confident these metrics would not be nearly as strong without proactive, thoughtful leadership meetings that address the issues—both the important and the urgent—that our organization faces.

And with that, the defense rests.

RUNNING MEETINGS THAT LACK FOCUS ON THE TOP PRIORITY

Scott Ault, Executive Vice President, Workplace Solutions, Mutual of Omaha

If there is one thing that drives me crazy as the leader of a large organization, it is unproductive or unnecessary meetings. Having talked to executive peers and leaders in other industries and companies, I know I am not alone in this.

I started my career in the insurance industry as a sales rep and have spent most of my career in jobs that have clear, direct sales quotas. These jobs have always come with great rewards if the quotas are achieved—and a corresponding "opportunity" to pursue job options elsewhere if they are not. Because of that intense focus on the goals and the ramifications for failure, I've tried hard to avoid unproductive meetings that don't get me closer to my goals.

Likewise, when I became a sales manager and later a director and vice president of sales, the focus was similarly clear. I coached my sales teams always to keep their eye on the prize, eliminate distractions, and make sure every action is in some way moving the ball down the field toward the goal line.

As I moved into more senior positions, I started spending more and more time at the main office, and my days started to fill with meetings and requests for my time that were not necessarily aligned to our most important goals. Then, when I took my current position, leading the largest organization I have ever been responsible for, I realized this was true even for the meetings *I* was responsible for: the meetings of my executive team. How did this happen?

I think I know the answer.

Working in a sales organization is a lot like playing on a golf team: Golfers have their individual scores, they are clear on what they are trying to achieve individually, and at the end of the match they add up the scores to see who won. On a football team, on the other hand, players are interdependent, and different players in different positions must work together to achieve the goal of winning a game and ultimately a championship. While different in the level of dependence and the teamwork required to win, both types of teams are absolutely clear about their goals.

I suspected that was why our meetings were not as productive and useful as they needed to be: I went from leading a golf team (a sales organization) to leading a football team (an organization with many different functions), but it took me a while to see that the goals for this new kind of team, in my new organization, were unclear. Like a football team, we needed an overall goal—one that would be shared at every level, across the organization. My mistake was not identifying that goal for the organization and then making sure everyone knew it and was aligned around it.

Once my team and I realized this and worked together to create our number one priority—our thematic goal—we built a meeting structure and cadence that would align to it. It included different types of meetings for different purposes—check-in meetings, weekly staff meetings, ad hoc meetings, quarterly meetings—as outlined in Patrick Lencioni's book *Death by Meeting*. My team and I also created additional meetings to communicate and reinforce the newly created thematic goal for the entire business, adding monthly meetings for leaders across the enterprise and all-hands meetings for the organization, to make sure everyone both understood and felt ownership for that most important organizational goal.

That may seem like a lot of meetings, but when they are aligned to the achievement of your most important goal, they are absolutely worth it. The success we have had in our organization since we implemented this highly aligned meeting approach has proved that to be true.

Since the primary goal is communicated and shared throughout the organization, all meetings are evaluated with respect to our primary goal. Meetings that are not aligned are examined, and in many cases canceled, thus returning to employees the one resource that can't be replaced: time.

With this kind of clarity, individual meeting requests or appointments also are more easily evaluated and, if they fail the "alignment" test, denied. While we value open communication and time spent with people both inside and outside of our organization, that could be done in many ways other than one-on-one appointments. I began encouraging my leaders to take that same approach, telling them I'd rather have a healthy, successful, aligned organization with people mad at us for not taking one-on-one meetings than to have an unhealthy, unsuccessful organization where we hold all meetings that are requested.

Clarity on our most important thematic goal has helped us reduce the number of unnecessary, unproductive, sometimes crazy-making meetings in our organization. For leaders looking to avoid my early mistake, I highly recommend this same approach: Develop your top priority, and align a meeting structure to it.

RUNNING MEETINGS WITHOUT PRODUCTIVE CONFLICT

Steve Long, Senior Vice President and General Manager, Commercial Business, Lenovo

I am Latin. Although I was born in the United States, I have made my home in two countries in Latin America and have worked, traveled, and spent significant time in most of the others. At the risk of stereotyping a whole subcontinent, my experience is that many people who live in that broad, diverse region are passionate and enjoy a good argument with friendly confrontation. I am no exception.

Perhaps that's why I truly love to mix it up—to challenge ideas and debate opinions. I enjoy a good disagreement and embrace constructive conflict. That is true at home and at work—and is definitely at its peak during the World Cup, which is distracting me as I write this.

A second thing that is true about me is that I have an extremely strong bias for action. I like to make decisions quickly, and once they are made, I like to go full speed, implementing the decision with pace and urgency—knowing we may have to course-correct along the way.

With these two things in mind, along with the well-known Intel mantra *Disagree and commit*, it's no wonder that I found a professional home at Intel and stayed there for 24 years.

If you have worked in technology anytime during the past half century, you have probably heard the phrase *Disagree and commit* many times. Coined first by Andy Grove—an Intel cofounder and long-time CEO, and a true icon in the technology world—that mantra is repeated and practiced daily throughout the tech industry and by countless organizations in other industries. The concept encourages disagreement and good, productive conflict, but only *prior* to a decision being made. After that decision becomes final, regardless of people's rival opinions and opposing positions previously, everybody must commit to it. Everyone must leave the meeting or conversation aligned. It helps leaders and teams avoid the "consensus trap," where the lack of consensus could lead to inaction. Following the *Disagree and commit* mantra also makes sure everyone is able to weigh in on an effort to make the best decision possible.

An important component to this principle is that the "disagree" must come *before* the "commit"—and therein was my mistake.

Although I had been using the phrase and practicing this approach with teams since I started working at Intel in 2000, I failed to deploy it when I took on my first executive leadership position at the company: as vice president and general manager for Intel Latin America in late 2010. My task was to drive results, and to do that, I decided the region needed a simplified strategy.

Notice what I said there: "*I* decided."

I had inherited a large team full of people who were, in most cases, older and more experienced than I was. Many had previously been my peers, and some had even been my senior leaders years before, yet they were now all reporting to me as members of my staff.

The problem was not with the strategy I had inherited. The team had spent considerable time on it, and it was a good, solid strategy despite being presented in a complex way. The problem was with rallying, communicating, and conquering the hearts of the broader sales team.

To solve that problem, I focused on simplifying the strategy and tactics, and then framing it simply with key numbers: 9–3–1, for $9 billion in revenue, three key strategies to get us there, and one unified team. When my staff eventually bought in, it helped focus and pave the way to achieve our key business metrics. The buy-in took longer than it needed to, however, because I failed to solicit my new leaders' opinions and ideas before moving forward.

Looking back, it seems so obvious. But why didn't I follow proper *Disagree and commit* protocol at the time?

Maybe I wanted to make a statement and demonstrate my authority as the new *jefe* ("boss") in charge, especially given past reporting relationships. Or could I have been concerned that the leadership team was too enamored with the complexity of the prior approach and would be resistant to change? Was it about my own overdeveloped bias for wanting immediate action? Or was I perhaps trying to save the expenses of flying in 15 leaders from across Latin America for just one meeting, when we were set to meet already at the sales kickoff in just a few weeks?

More than likely it was a combination of all these, paired with the fact that with limited time before our sales kickoff, I wanted to put a plan in place. The important point here, however, is that I did not ask for the team's input. Nor did I honor their wealth of experience as I should have. Instead, I pulled the content together and presented it to the organization in our sales kickoff without getting the senior leaders' full buy-in. While the broader organization rallied—there was no chance for the leadership team to disagree—as you might expect, a mixed sense of commitment followed.

I can only imagine the colorful names I was called in a variety of languages, probably deservedly so, by my new team within that first month of my new job!

Bottom line: I blew it. I had to unwind, take a step back, and recoil before moving forward. Only when I admitted the mistake with the direct team and allowed the debate to happen, did the leadership team make great strides toward a commitment to achieve the 9–3–1 plan.

I recently took on a new role at Lenovo as general manager of the commercial business. My organization and its goals are significant, and my team is incredibly diverse. Having learned from the mistake described earlier, I try hard now to slow down—to allow productive debate and to practice real *Disagree and commit* protocol whenever a big decision must be made. This is even more important with a truly international team, spanning multiple continents and representing different cultures with different comfort levels with respect to conflict and debate—I've learned that I must be sensitive to these differences as I lead my organization.

My hope is that the leaders in my organization will not repeat the mistake I made with my new team in Latin America many years ago. If they allow for disagreeing and *then* committing as they and their teams make important decisions for the good of the organization, I am confident we will have better meetings, better decisions, and greater organizational success.

RUNNING MEETINGS THAT FAIL TO CLARIFY DECISIONS AND ACTIONS

Richard Brilliant, Chief Risk and Compliance Officer, Carnival Corporation

Every day, on the bridge of every one of the 91 ships in our fleet across all nine Carnival Corporation cruise line brands, the ship engineers practice closed-loop communication.

"Five degrees to port," says the navigator.

"Five degrees to port," the helmsman repeats.

"Yes," the navigator replies.

Closed-loop communication is a simple but effective communication technique used to avoid misunderstandings. When the sender gives a message, the receiver repeats it back verbatim. The sender then confirms the message by using the word *yes* or *confirmed.* If the receiver incorrectly repeats the message, the sender replies with the word *negative* and then repeats the process until there is no ambiguity. Only then are appropriate actions taken.

Clarity of communication on the bridge is paramount, a nonnegotiable for the officers and seamen navigating our ships. The safety of our passengers and our crew depends upon it. Likewise, clarity is critical when the captain of each ship leads his daily meeting with his team of officers, all of whom are facing different challenges and different problems every day.

The captain's top priorities—what keeps him or her up at night—are safety and schedule. Keeping the passengers and crew safe is first and foremost, but getting our vessel where it needs to be on time is another high priority. Not only is the failure to stay on schedule a customer service issue, but there are also significant costs associated with being late into or out of port.

The cruise director's top priority, on the other hand, has always been making sure our guests are having fun and are entertained. And how does one have fun on one of our ships? Eating, drinking, gaming, dancing, educational events, beauty treatments, and fitness classes are just a few of the many ways our guests enjoy themselves while on board.

The responsibilities and daily priorities of these two key officers, as well as the others in that meeting, can be vastly different at times, but all are tasked with a common goal: taking care of the people on board. That's why it is critical that before their daily meeting is over, they leave with perfect alignment about decisions and actions.

I'd like to report that over the course of my career as a leader, I have always ended meetings with absolute clarity about decisions and actions—but that wouldn't be true.

Early in my career, I was promoted to my first significant leadership role, moving from an individual contributor role to a manager of audit services. As is true in many cases, I was promoted due to my skill and expertise in my functional area, not my experience leading people and certainly not because I ran great meetings.

As a new leader with no training, little guidance, and few great meeting role models, I ran meetings that not only were boring and lacked focus, but often ended in confusion. This led to misunderstandings between members of my staff, introduced delays and mistakes, and sometimes meant extra work was required by my team in getting audits completed. And as you might expect, my internal customer relationships suffered. Levels of engagement and morale among the people I was leading were lower than anticipated.

I've learned over time that forcing clarity, especially with respect to roles, appropriate behaviors, communications, and decisions made in meetings, is a key leadership responsibility. As my responsibilities have grown, the risks associated with a lack of clarity have grown dramatically as well. Mistakes due to confusion on the part of the organization that I now lead as chief risk and compliance officer, can result in safety issues, regulatory and compliance problems, and significant fines for the organization—all of which are unacceptable outcomes.

We simply can't put our guests or employees in jeopardy because we communicated poorly.

One simple meeting protocol we follow religiously to ensure excellence in communication is especially effective: We save the final five minutes of every staff meeting to restate the decisions and actions, and to note who is responsible for each. Although it may sound simple and obvious, my experience is that more often than not, this last step is needed to clarify a key point or assignment decision. That simple practice allows for greater alignment of my leadership team as we disembark for our next meeting and ensures better alignment across my department going forward.

To close the loop on this, I'll offer one final communication in hopes of avoiding confusion: "As leaders, we should always end our meetings with clarity."

"As leaders, we should always end our meetings with clarity."

"Yes."

ENDING MEETINGS WITHOUT CLEAR MESSAGING

Marc Cameron, Senior Vice President, Resources Industries Sales, Services, and Technology, Caterpillar (written when Managing Director of Rio Tinto Kennecott Copper)

Safety. It has always been our most important focus at Rio Tinto Kennecott Copper, and it is embedded in everything we do. It's not only our first core value and number one priority, but it is an important component in all of our key strategies and decisions.

We track safety incidents very closely, and when an incident occurs, we take it personally as a leadership team and across the organization. Although we strive to avoid all incidents completely, in a business like ours, 100 percent success at all times is an especially challenging aspiration. When incidents do occur, we spend a lot of time deconstructing what went wrong—what we might've done better—to ensure we avoid similar incidents in the future.

If you don't care about safety and are not willing to commit to continuous improvement and focus in this area, you're not going to be happy working at Rio Tinto. And, truth be told, if you don't care about safety, we don't want you here.

Across the Rio Tinto enterprise, and specifically here at Kennecott Copper, we start every meeting with a "zero harm" share about health and safety so that it is top of mind right from the start. And, while the safety focus is absolutely critical, we also have to have clarity about the other business issues we will be discussing so that upon leaving the meeting, we are able to ensure the organization is aligned and informed with respect to our plans and decisions.

As a professional engineer, my functional area of expertise has been marked by precision, design, logic, and great attention to detail. This is what engineers do best. What we generally are not known for, however, is our outstanding communication skills—and I am no exception. Communicating effectively and repeatedly has always been an area of continuous personal improvement. But in my role with Kennecott Copper, with the safety of over 2,000 employees and contractors in jeopardy, there is no place for a communication breakdown. The impact on our people and their families, friends, and loved ones due to a significant incident is at stake, and there is no room for me to communicate poorly.

Recognizing my personal challenges in this area, I discussed the issue with my executive team and we agreed we could all do better. We needed to improve as a team and put a process in place to make sure to leave our meetings knowing what we decided and what we would be communicating as *one voice* with our extended teams. We brought in an expert in this area who presented a proven model and structure for better meetings, which required ending with clarity and cascading messages, but I also dug deep into my personal experience for a technique to fine-tune the approach.

I recalled something I learned while playing and coaching hockey: The best hockey coaches were always willing to stop play right in the middle of practice to ensure the agreed-upon practice plan was being executed correctly. In fact, the best coaches had no problem stopping play multiple times to ensure the team knew exactly what was supposed to be happening at every moment on the ice. Stopping to point out a play that was run well was a great way to reinforce the behavior and increase skill and the likelihood of success. Likewise, stopping play in a practice when things went poorly had an equally powerful instructive effect. Clearly communicating what went wrong and what could be improved kept the team and players from making the same error again. When direction was given and repeated, there was no mistake about who should be doing what, out on the ice. Overcommunication brought clarity, helped get the most out of our limited ice time at our practices, and ultimately helped us win more games.

As my executive team implemented our new meeting structure and cadence, I decided to deploy this same strategy. With many important things to discuss, our weekly meetings were often long, and it was easy to lose track of decisions and commitments if there wasn't this consistent, deliberate focus. I decided I would stop every meeting three specific times to summarize and reconfirm the decisions and actions made. And three is just the minimum. The team and I agreed anyone can stop the meeting to check commitments and corresponding messages as often as necessary, in order to improve communication during and, importantly, after our meetings. The results have been dramatic.

Since deploying these measures and being more deliberate about our messaging, we have received a lot of great qualitative feedback about the better and clearer messages coming out of our team meetings. The engineer in me loves data and metrics, though, and I am happy to report that since being so focused on communication, many of the key business metrics we watch carefully—including employee engagement levels and Net Promoter Scores—are up significantly. And, most importantly, our metrics regarding our top priority, safety, improved at the same time, with the number of incidents and corresponding absentee rates dropping to near-historic lows.

The mining business is not a game. But I am grateful for the lessons I learned from my past coaches about how best to communicate and win in our business.

MISTAKE #4

Hiring Fast, Firing Slow

Great vision without great people is irrelevant.
—Jim Collins

HIRING FAST, FIRING SLOW

"Darlin', let's go celebrate!" I shouted as I walked in the door, having just returned from a business trip. "I got a promotion!"

At least I thought it was a promotion . . .

I had been working for a software company as an executive leader responsible for sales and support across a large US and international geography. While I was on that business trip, our company's CEO and COO called me out of the blue to ask whether I would take on an additional sales unit. They shared that our company needed growth. Of course, it did. I had never known a for-profit company that didn't. But growth was especially important to our company in the year ahead, they said, encouraging me to build a new team of "hunters": people who would go after key accounts that had never done business with our organization before.

I would have a sizeable training and education budget to work with, could hire a sales director to run that new unit, and would be authorized to hire as many as 10 new salespeople (and pay them extremely well) right out of the gate. And apparently, I was the exact guy they wanted for this important role.

A salesperson, if you don't already know, is the easiest person in the world to sell to. My wife reminded me that the position, which promised both additional responsibility and a lot of additional work, came with no promise of more money and with much greater risk than my current position. But flattering me as the "exact guy" worked—I said yes, right then and there on that call.

I hired a sales director I knew and trusted, and we got to work building the team of hunters. Knowing the historical ramp time for salespeople in our company, and knowing also the length of our typical sales cycle, we had to move fast in building our team. And the repeated calls from the CEO regarding the status of hiring added to the pressure to hire and hire fast.

You already know where this is going.

The sales director and I had about 20 years of collective leadership experience between us, and we absolutely knew that we should hire with close attention to our corporate culture and fit. But we didn't.

We knew that we should check references—a whole lot of them—and really get to know these candidates. But we didn't do that either.

And we knew that hiring super quickly when you're desperate was a bad idea. But in a tight labor market with a big bogey and limited time to achieve it, we did just that.

The results were predictable: weak employees, poor results, and the intense, multiple, recurring headaches that hiring the wrong employees invariably cause. The worst of the hires turned out to be professional sales job seekers—not workers, but *seekers*. These were total scam artists who faked their history, set up phone numbers and fake business names, and acted as one another's key references while taking on multiple jobs and milking the companies for money until they were discovered. They preyed on leaders like us who were so desperate to hire that we cut corners on hiring, rushed the process, and ultimately got exactly what we deserved.

Our team of hunters didn't make the quota that year (shocking!) and our jobs were spared due to a large, last-minute deal that made the numbers respectable. That deal was closed by an employee who had come over from another business unit—someone who had been hired the right way, with the right timing, and for the right reasons.

So embarrassing.

There may be no other type of leadership mistake that is so common and causes such a visceral reaction in leaders than the mistakes made with respect to hiring and firing. You show me an experienced leader *without* a couple of stories about hiring or firing poorly, and I will tell you what I call that leader: *liar*.

With so many examples of leaders who made mistakes around hiring and firing, it was hard to choose the ones to highlight in the pages that follow. But the seven chosen leaders not only have great stories about mistakes regarding hiring and firing, but have smart ideas on things to remember at both the front end and the back end of the employee life cycle.

HIRING WITHOUT ALIGNMENT TO PURPOSE

Christine Talbot, Senior Vice President, Human Resources,
World Vision, US (retired)

At World Vision, we have always been very clear about who we are. It is front and center on our website, in all of our communications internally, and reiterated with partners and donors: "World Vision is a Christian humanitarian organization dedicated to working with children, families, and their communities worldwide to reach their full potential by tackling the causes of poverty and injustice." And around the world, the organization's vision is communicated and lived every day in the 100 countries where our employees and partners work to reach our goal: "life in all its fullness for every child."

During my time as the senior executive of human resources, it was my responsibility to see that we supported the organization's talent needs, spanning all phases of engagement through the full life cycle of a staff member. This included recruiting, hiring, onboarding, training, managing performance and benefits, and finally retirement from the organization. Meeting the needs for talent is one of the most critical tasks of an organization, and getting it right on the front end in selection of talent is paramount—arguably the most important part of the talent equation. I learned this the hard way as an executive leader at a previous employer.

When I was a senior leader at a major not-for-profit healthcare system whose technology requirements and complexities were growing exponentially, we needed to hire a number of senior technology leaders to fill a critical gap in our organization. The right candidates would need to have great technology expertise; be experienced in managing large technical units in an organization, as well as with many complex technical projects; and be adept at building an organization capable of meeting both our immediate technology needs and those in the future for the whole hospital system. As we interviewed multiple candidates, only a few stood out as meeting all of *those* criteria. But there was one criterion we didn't consider enough: The candidate needed to be aligned with our purpose.

After hiring several new executive leaders who could meet our immediate technology needs, we soon learned that they lacked passion for the mission of the organization, for our industry, and for patient care. Although we recognized the misalignment relatively quickly, we discovered as time went on that it was a larger mistake than we first knew. Our new leaders had already hired a lot of "their" people (as senior leaders often do), most of whom were unfamiliar with the inner workings of not-for-profit companies. These were smart people who were skilled and excited to participate in the building out of new technology, but like the new leaders who hired them, they cared very little about the mission.

Seeking to be successful, they moved quickly to get results, often without pausing to gain an appreciation for the history, mission, and broader interest of the organization. And with no tie to the business and its purpose, only to the technology, these new hires often left abruptly when exciting projects ended or when they were recruited to better-paying opportunities elsewhere.

The churn of leadership turnover, change, and constant adaptation resulted in uncertainty, chaos, jockeying for approval, and general distraction. The HR organization was pressed to support a leadership team divided by old and new, by mission-focused staff and those focused on individual success. The predictable result was expensive turnover and strained internal relationships across divisions. As a leader charged with oversight of the hiring, I felt keenly the pain of these challenges and the selection mismatches.

When I came to World Vision in early 2015, I was determined not to commit that same mistake.

I was happy that the World Vision purpose was a critical part of my screening before I was hired. Rich Stearns, the CEO who would be my manager, interviewed me in the executive conference room, where pictures of the poor with whom he had personally interacted lined the walls. As a decade-long World Vision child sponsor, I was already "in" on the mission to some degree. But my visit to the headquarters and that interview with Rich—including his tears as he spoke of those served by World Vision, sharing some of the unique stories of hope and transformation behind those photos on the walls—cemented my desire to join the mission of serving the poor around the world.

At World Vision, while we focus on fit from a purpose and values standpoint for every hire, we are especially careful when we hire leaders. It's not that we value people differently; as a Christian organization we believe that every person is created in God's image and that we are all equal. But in a large organization, when you hire a leader—especially a senior leader who will be representing the company and hiring many employees—the impact of misaligned hiring can be exponential, and even more so in a mission-driven organization.

Typically, leaders hired from for-profit environments take a significant downshift from robust compensation packages in order to serve with us. This often acts as an initial filter. Our rigorous approach to hiring leaders includes three additional criteria that we use as filters in the process. First, in addition to functional area competency, managers must have a servant leadership approach to their staff. Second, the right leaders must have a passion for our purpose, along with a willingness to dedicate their professional life to helping the poor, including an expectation and openness to the transformation of one's own understanding of God's heart when it comes to the poor. And finally, leaders must be aligned to our Christian values; they must be willing and able to integrate our shared faith into their leadership mindsets and behaviors, and to consciously live out our core values.

We applied that same rigorous hiring process to our most important position of all: a new CEO to replace Rich Stearns, who had successfully and faithfully led our organization for 20 years. The board of directors, which was responsible for the hire, applied those same criteria to ensure the right fit, sifting through hundreds of impressive prospects to come up with a slate of candidates. The final result was an outstanding hire for the future of our organization: Edgar Sandoval, a true servant leader who had lived our purpose and had demonstrated his commitment to it during his previous three years as World Vision's chief operating officer.

Having worked alongside Edgar for those past few years, I knew he was the right fit for the position and his alignment to our purpose was clear and would have the best possible impact on the organization. Indeed, he has continued to live our purpose and demonstrate it, both across and outside of the organization, on a daily basis. What's more, with his leadership, every future hire that World Vision makes will represent a focus on that same purpose: helping individuals and communities lift themselves out of poverty.

HIRING WITHOUT ALIGNMENT TO VALUES

Duncan Richardson, Cofounder and President, Bodies in Motion; Business Broker, Laska Company

All four of my kids—ages 21, 18, 16, and 14—are black belts in Taekwondo. I guess that's not too surprising given that my wife, Rachel, and I are black belt master instructors who run a small business called Bodies in Motion, where we teach Taekwondo to hundreds of people each year. Regardless of their "unfair advantage" in achieving that designation, each of the four kids put in years of hard work to achieve that level of expertise, and we are super proud of them. As a family, some of the things that are important to us include having fun, being disciplined and fit, and caring for and about others. These values also align nicely to some of the core values of our business: commitment to work, commitment to guests, and fun.

Rachel and I started The Academy of Taekwondo 23 years ago, after graduating from Boise State University. She was a cheerleader, and I was the mascot, Buster Bronco, on the sidelines of all the Boise State football games. (Go Broncos!) With our passion for the martial arts and exercise in general, and our shared preference for constant activity, we should have known that the more traditional, more sedentary jobs we took immediately after college would never be a fit. That's how we ended up starting our own Taekwondo studio that, over time, became Bodies in Motion.

One thing we did know was that if we were going to grow our business to scale, we needed great people who aligned to our values and would delight our customers. But as our business gained traction, and grew from the two of us to a team of three and then four, on its way to the dozens of employees we have today, we started having trouble hiring great people. We took care as owners to do well at hiring, but still we were at about a 60/40 split between *great* employees that we would *absolutely* rehire given the chance, and *good* employees that we would *probably* rehire. I suppose that's a mistake on its own. But my real mistake was not having a strong process to know in advance that the candidates were *absolutely* a great fit.

Having heard stories of companies like Southwest Airlines, Nordstrom, and Zappos working hard to find the right candidates and taking clever approaches in their interviewing process, we developed our own creative approach. The purpose was to make sure anyone we hired, now or in the future, would align to the two most important values from our perspective: commitment to guests and fun.

It turns out those are also the most difficult values to discern in an interview.

After some trial and error with our process, we found an approach that works well to this day. It starts with a group interview, although we don't go out of our way to make applicants aware of that as we schedule them in. This is the first of many fun surprises in our process for hiring camp counselors as well as other team members.

The organizer encourages this group of applicants to introduce themselves to one another and then to ask each other questions for approximately 20 minutes prior to the start of the actual interview. What the applicants don't realize, however, is that the interview has already begun. Along with real candidates in this "get to know you" conversation are several "motioneers" in disguise—our employees, pretending to be candidates. They use this time to determine the applicants' ability to have fun, be kind, and treat people with respect.

I never want to miss part one of these interviews—for many reasons, but the best one is the look on the candidates' faces when the leader of the process says, "Will all the motioneers in the group please step forward?" Priceless.

Part two of the group interview includes "speed-dating" questions, with motioneers and the candidates moving around quickly in an effort to get to know one another. Creative questions like *Tell me about your favorite book, but do it in a pirate voice* are critical to this part of the interview; they help us discern the applicants' activity levels and the ways they make fun.

Part three is a mock birthday party, where two candidates at a time are instructed to perform an impromptu skit in front of the rest of the group, who pretend to be birthday party guests. The purpose is to see how the candidates might make a spontaneous situation fun and show how they might entertain our guests—whether at a birthday party, working at the front desk, as a barista in our coffee shop, or as a fitness instructor. This interview process might sound awful to you—and if so, you need not apply!

By the time these steps in the interview process are complete, some of the applicants have backed out or been disqualified. Next, we do more formal interviews with those who remain—yet even the formal interviews are designed to check for fun, commitment to guests, and now also commitment to work. We screen finalists for these key qualities in other ways as well, such as asking for the references that *we* want (based on their stories, their history, and their answers to our questions) rather than the ones *they* might want to provide. Because this usually catches them off guard, we get a more accurate assessment of who they are as candidates.

Does your hiring process allow for clearly identifying candidates who match up with the values that are most important to your business? If not, start by discerning what your company sees as the most important values—and the most difficult values to hire for. Then, find a way to aggressively and thoroughly screen for those values. It can make a big difference, ensuring that all your employees are *great* ones whom you would *absolutely* hire again. These are the employees who will help you put your business in motion to achieve great things.

HIRING WITHOUT ALIGNMENT TO CULTURAL FIT

Alex Potts, President Emeritus, Buckingham Strategic Wealth; Former CEO, Loring Ward; Author of *The Wealth Solution*

I've heard it said that culture trumps strategy. In fact, renowned management consultant Peter Drucker purportedly took it one step further, saying, "Culture eats strategy for breakfast." Smart guy.

I think we all can agree that a sound business strategy is critical if we want our organization to succeed. In fact, in my business I have relied on people who are much smarter than I am to help determine that strategy. But culture is a completely different issue. As CEO, I have to take responsibility for the culture, and I can't give that responsibility to anyone else. I consider myself not only the chief *executive* officer but the chief *culture* officer as well. Culture is *that* important.

To establish a healthy organizational culture, two things are critical: an aligned, example-led leadership team and clarity about what is most important to your business. Several years ago, I made a mistake on both of these fronts, and everyone involved suffered.

I had a key opening on my executive team, one that was going to be important to both the short-term key initiatives and the long-term success of the business. Unfortunately, I hadn't realized then what I now know: You need to identify and be clear about your core values *before* you hire a key executive. Any hiring completed before you identify those values leaves success up to chance.

As we moved through the interview process for this key leader, one candidate stood out as the smartest, most strategic of the lot. He had worked at great companies and had done great things. His expertise and experience would surely help us overcome the challenges our business was facing. My other leaders and I noticed a few small red flags—things that would have been glaring sirens if we had previously identified our values and used them appropriately as a filter for these executive candidates. But instead of paying attention to these red flags (and disqualifiers, I am now certain), we hired him.

Almost immediately, my previously strong executive team began to weaken. Unexpected in-fighting led to issues in trust and confidence among peers. The newborn lack of trust on the executive team then started to cascade throughout the organization. Although the business was strong at that moment, I could see politics and confusion were becoming more prevalent, and I knew the strength of our business wouldn't last without regaining alignment on my team. Anyone could see that our team was in trouble and needed help getting back on track.

I brought in a key advisor—someone I had known for more than 40 years—and we began dissecting the problem. The advisor started by sharing with me some hard truths about my team and business. One of his especially poignant observations was that we would continue to have similar issues if we didn't set about the business of clarifying our values.

So, we got busy.

After two full days of hard work, among other key outcomes, we had finally identified those core values: humble, caring, and "smart-do." The first two values are self-explanatory; smart-do relates to a combination of intellectual and situational/people smarts, and the willingness and can-do attitude to figure things out to get things done.

As part of that off-site event, we determined that these values should be used not only to hire great people who would fit with our culture, but to move people out of the business who did not fit. We also discussed that if our executive team was not living and demonstrating those values daily, the new values would mean nothing to the organization, and there would be no point even to sharing them with our extended teams.

We finally had the clarity we needed on values. We also realized that this recently hired executive (who actually attended the off-site and helped define the core values!) was a poor choice and would have to leave the company.

What's more, having applied those values as a filter across the whole executive team, it became apparent that there were actually *two* executive leaders on the team who were not a fit. If these were truly behaviors we absolutely wouldn't compromise on, they both would have to go.

Unfortunately, due to business realities and other extenuating circumstances, it took longer than it should have to move both of those executives off the team and out of the company. (That's probably another mistake!) The increasing challenges and pain the company felt throughout the extended termination process proved a great example of why hiring with alignment to core values is so critical.

After the termination of those two leaders, we made replacements to the executive team with two new individuals who are humble and caring, and who exhibit the smart-do attitude that we had determined is so important. The team is more cohesive and more trusting. The business is stronger. And the leaders and I talk about the importance of our core values with every opportunity.

I can say with all honesty that the values now are fully steeped into our culture. Clear and concise, these values are our proverbial North Star and inform our hiring, successes, failures, and improvements within the business. Those values also serve to protect the most important component in our business: our culture.

HIRING DESPITE RED FLAGS

Nick Schichtle, Founder and CEO, Search Insights CPT

As a young leader, still relatively new to the recruiting industry, I secured approval from the senior executives to hire two additional positions to take advantage of favorable market conditions. Our industry is a leading economic indicator, and this was one of those times when the market was especially strong. Unfortunately, that meant the demand for the subject matter experts I needed was high, while supply was low.

I was thrilled to find two strong candidates who exceeded my requirements and expectations. I felt I should move quickly before competition for them escalated, and because I had an elevated target to meet.

Both candidates cruised through the interview process, as both women were polished, professional, and proven. Add to that the huge plus that they would be able to hit the ground running—this was crucial for me as I needed to minimize ramp time, considering our clock was ticking toward our fiscal year end. Executive leadership expected results.

As I prepared the offer letters and reflected on the multiple conversations and interviews I had with each, something wasn't sitting well with me about my interactions with one of the candidates, Linda. Despite her exceptional credentials, she was verbose. Her explanations and examples during interviews had gone on a bit too long, and she hadn't responded to the verbal and nonverbal cues from me and others. Having committed similar transgressions in the past myself, I quickly convinced myself this was something that could be overcome with coaching.

After I expressed my intentions of making an offer, she felt compelled to continue to convince me, at length, that I was making the right decision. Eager to complete the process, I chalked it up to passion, energy, and excitement to join the team and contribute.

In reality, these issues pointed to a situational awareness problem, a concept I had experience with while playing quarterback at Oregon State in the late 1980s. Good quarterbacks at the Division I level need to have acute situational awareness in order to recognize blitzes, alter pass protections, change plays at the line of scrimmage, or simply throw the football away to keep a drive alive or avoid a turnover.

Although situational awareness wasn't in the job description, in hindsight I knew it was critical for success at multiple levels in the organization. If hired, Linda would interface with internal and external customers consistently. Yet we were in the final stages of the hiring process, and I needed to move forward without delay. So, despite these seemingly minor red flags, I made the decision to go ahead with the hire instead of investigating these concerns further.

It ended up costing me dearly.

Initial feedback was overwhelmingly positive as colleagues started to experience Linda's obvious strengths. But it didn't take long for the same red flags I saw to surface. A few months in, I realized the magnitude of my error. Under the pressure of goals, a desire to impress, colleague competition, and the need to achieve quickly, Linda gave explanations that grew only *longer* under stress, adding to her intensity and verbosity. My coaching and personal experience in this area made little difference in curbing her behavior and its impact, thus harming both me and our business dearly—with strained customer relationships, lost productivity, missed targets, challenges among my team members, and questions from my senior leaders. I had to move her off my team and eventually out of the company.

The embarrassing and ironic part of this was that my own lack of situational awareness had prevented me from making the right adjustments prior to hiring. In the decades that have followed, I have come to zero in on the red flags that arise. Now I slow the decision process down to take the additional steps necessary to vet through concerns. Hiring too fast, in my experience, has proven to be a risk I can't afford to take.

HIRING WITHOUT ENSURING PEOPLE ARE IN THE RIGHT SEATS

Kathy Haney, Vice President, Human Resources, Griffin Media

In *Good to Great,* Jim Collins famously said that to build a strong organization you need to start by getting the right people on the bus. Staying with that metaphor, at Griffin Media we have been especially focused on why our "bus" exists: "To keep Oklahomans safe, informed, and entertained." And to Collins's point, getting the right people on our bus has been a big key to our success. Our four core values are humility, passion, positivity, and smart (people smart), and at the risk of violating that first value, we are proud of our success recruiting, hiring, onboarding, and managing performance based upon those four core values.

But getting people in the right *seats* is also critically important, and that's where we at times had previously missed the bus altogether. As Vice President of Human Resources, I have to take my share of the responsibility for this. And this mistake almost cost us a truly great team member who was not in the right seat to make use of his unique gifts.

When I first heard about Patrick Lencioni's book *The 6 Types of Working Genius,* I must admit to one of my first reactions: *Does the world really* need *another personality assessment?* I personally have taken and/or administered at least a dozen of these tools, and I think they all have merit, but I didn't see a need for another. After an introduction to this approach at an executive team off-site, however, I realized this one was different.

Rather than a personality assessment, this is more of a productivity tool, and as we learned about the tool together as an executive team, we immediately understood each other better through that productivity lens. Exploring what type of work *gives* each of us energy and what work *drains* our energy, and applying that knowledge, has had a profound effect on each member of our executive team personally, and on the cohesion of our team collectively. And as we've cascaded it throughout Griffin Media, it has had a profound effect on our whole organization.

On a personal basis, the tool helped me understand that while I get energy from evaluating situations, making decisions, and supporting people and initiatives (embodying the Genius Types of Discernment and Enablement), I can easily be drained of my energy if I spend too much time in the ideation phases of work (Wonder and Invention). No wonder (pun intended) it took so long to get the creative work related to developing a key initiative, The Griffin Advantage, off the ground! Only when I began leveraging team leaders who are more gifted in ideation than I am, did the program design really take off, gain momentum, and become the program we needed it to be.

It has been said that the best leaders are both vulnerable and self-aware, and this was a big learning opportunity not just for me but for our executive team as well. My willingness to admit the areas where I need help, and to leverage those in the organization who are more gifted than I am in certain situations, has led to a higher level of success.

We are fortunate to have extremely self-aware leaders at the top of our organization. Our CEO, David Griffin, is a great Discerner but recognizes he is not as gifted at Wonder and Invention. Saying,

"I don't need to be involved in creating the new set design, but let me know if I can help by providing input once you have concepts," is a recent example of how he understands both his skills and his limitations, allowing him to contribute where he might add the most value.

Wade Deaver, our president, is especially aware of the areas where he gets energy (Wonder and Tenacity) and how this can not only benefit the team but also cause challenges if his energy is not channeled appropriately. Asking, "Am I causing turbulence by moving too fast from Wonder to Tenacity?" and "Is my desire to close on this initiative helping or hurting the program?" are recent examples of his self-awareness.

Here are some other examples of applying this tool with our executive team:

- Pairing the right executives to lead our efforts to build a new broadcast set for our Oklahoma station News 9, by leveraging their combined unique gifts—Invention, Discernment, and Tenacity—to get the design right and complete the project on time and on budget.

- Leveraging another executive's gift of Wonder as a reminder for the team to consider where the business is headed and to ask good questions regarding how we might leverage market conditions and try new approaches for the good of the organization.

- Allowing a team member to leverage his passion for Galvanizing to rally our content team around maximizing our impact and growing market share.

- Putting each executive's Working Genius Type (instead of their organizational title) alongside their name on their office door.

Seeing the impact of this tool on our executive and director teams, we began cascading the approach throughout our organization as we manage performance, hire new employees, and staff projects. That's how we managed to retain a great team member recently, who was aligned to company values but on the verge of leaving the organization because his unique ideation gifts went unrecognized. Assessing Genius Types across the company and encouraging conversations about unique gifts in our regular review cycle enabled us to catch this mistake and correct it before the damage was done.

Considering Geniuses and Frustrations as one criterion when hiring for fit, in both the organization and the role, is now commonplace, and recently it helped us promote the right leader into her role as vice president of sales. As we identify our thematic goals and key initiatives, now we always consider fit related to this model as we pick a project leader and the right team to achieve the program's goals.

Having the right people in the right seats on our organizational bus now has us firing on all cylinders, on the road to keeping the great people of the state of Oklahoma safe, informed, and entertained. It turns out the world—and Griffin Media—really did need another assessment.

WAITING TOO LONG TO FIRE

Dave Parsin, Global Lead, Cloud Security Solutions and
Offensive Services, Bitdefender

Managing people can be messy. And I don't like messy.

I once used the miniature scissors on my Swiss Army knife to give a haircut to a friend. It took about two hours and involved three things that should have made for a disaster: a crazy swirl of wavy hair that had its way with my friend's head during his extended trip to Europe, a torrential rainstorm, and a little too much access to Italian wine prior to both the idea and execution of the cut. It took two hours because, as I mentioned, I don't like messy. I like precision—*measure twice, cut once*—and because I had never cut hair before.

I should also mention that it took two hours for *just one side of his head.* I had another friend with another Swiss Army knife working the other side. This other "stylist" is more of an artist and showed great flair but less precision during *his* inaugural haircut, which was done in about five minutes. Let the historical record show that the left side of the head—the side I was responsible for—proved to be the better cut for this particular head due to the care I took and the attention to detail I showed.

My love for detail (which goes hand in hand with my dislike of all things messy) started early and was validated and magnified when I enrolled at Stanford University. There, I played on the baseball team that won national championships in 1987 and 1988, in great part due to the precise execution of our practices, the study of the mechanics of the game, and the detailed analysis of the percentages and probabilities of the "game within the game." I majored in electrical engineering, which proved to be a great fit for me. Success in that subject, as in baseball, requires logic, precision, and accuracy—three things that were essential later when I headed to Harvard for my MBA and, eventually, as I began my professional career.

Upon graduating and joining the workforce, my attention to detail and passion for precision continued to serve me well as an individual contributor in a variety of technology organizations. Over time, though, my work responsibilities grew and moved me away from the comfort of binary technology and more toward the less comfortable and less precise responsibilities of leading people and managing teams. Managing talent in an organization is the opposite of binary; hiring, giving regular constructive feedback, promotions, and so forth, all fall into varying categories of gray—colors that I find messy!

Perhaps the messiest gray of all came when my job required me to move people out of the organization (that is, to fire them). I found myself delaying as I wondered about my own performance: Had I had given enough feedback to the employee prior to the termination conversation? Had I shared my disappointment with them regarding their work? Did I leave them to work their way through difficult situations all alone instead of offering the guidance a good leader should? My academic degrees taught me little (if anything) about firing employees who did not perform or proved to be a poor fit. I was out of my league, and the mistakes started adding up.

Over the years, I discovered there were many reasons I conducted those end-of-employee-life-cycle issues poorly. The first was that I find confrontation uncomfortable. I am pretty easygoing, both as a guy and as a manager. Giving criticism doesn't come easily.

Another reason I wasn't great at firing people was that I know the difficulty of finding replacements for key positions, especially during a strong economy. Good workers aren't always ready to leave their positions, and there is great expense to bringing on a new employee. So I second-guessed myself: Would it be easier just to keep who we have?

I also knew that releasing an employee oftentimes brought drama that took its toll on the team. Would the team be strong enough to weather this type of big interruption?

And finally, firing felt like a confirmation of my own failures in hiring and managing this employee—something that was hard to admit.

More recently, when I served in an executive sales position, it became clear that someone on my team needed to be released due to poor performance. My team was suffering because they had a colleague who wasn't a fit and wasn't doing his share of the work. As before, I began second-guessing the costs of removing him from the team and briefly considered delaying the termination, this time due to the great demands on quarterly results and my fears that they would be in jeopardy.

But this time I resisted the urge to delay and instead moved quickly. By cutting ties with appropriate speed, I freed up not only my time and my mindshare (this had been weighing on me heavily), but also those of the rest of my team. The team expressed relief about the change, and individual contributions picked up across the team. In the end, we were able to achieve our objectives.

As leaders, it is our responsibility to offer regular, customized feedback to each team member so there is the opportunity to grow within the workplace. By taking immediate action in this instance, I demonstrated to the rest of my team not only that each of us would be held accountable for our actions and results, but that all of us would be validated for the good work, creativity, and resourcefulness we each brought to the team.

Once it becomes clear a team member is not a good fit, the right thing to do is to make a swift extraction. Being decisive about releasing a poorly performing employee can demonstrate your willingness to do the difficult things you need to do as a leader to make the team better.

TAKING TOO LONG TO OVERHAUL THE EXECUTIVE TEAM

Andy Heily, President and CEO, The Krusteaz Company

"What's the best team you've ever been on?" the consultant asked my executive team on the first day of our two-day off-site event.

For me, the answer was easy: my college cross-country team at Georgetown in the mid-1990s.

"What made it great?" the consultant asked next.

Also easy: We valued team over self. We had clarity on a singular goal—winning the NCAA championship. We spent time together, knew each other, and cared about each other. We pushed each other and leveraged one another's strengths and weaknesses. We won.

I could go on—and I did. It was fun talking about that team; it took me back to a great time of growth, comradery, and success.

Next question: "What would happen if *this* team—this executive team—became the best team any of us has ever been on?"

This time the whole team responded: We would care more about the organization than our departments. Company direction, priorities, and strategy would be clear. Fewer politics and less confusion would reign in our organization. We'd be a talent magnet in the industry, and our retention of great people would improve. Revenue and profit would increase. We would win more often. We'd have more fun.

The answers to the two questions were eerily similar. Yet it was clear to me, and probably to everyone in the room, that we were a long way from being that best team.

The team assessment we took, based on Patrick Lencioni's *The Five Dysfunctions of a Team*, confirmed that we had "opportunity" in all five behaviors of great teams: Trust, Conflict, Commitment, Accountability, and Results. We made commitments collectively and individually about improving upon those behaviors that needed attention if we were to achieve greatness. But the team in that original configuration never got there. Smart people, yes. Committed, yes. Willing to put the team above self and organization above department, no.

I've made many mistakes as a CEO (and continue to make them all the time), but the big one here is that I didn't move fast enough when it was clear this team could never become that great team the organization needed.

When I became CEO and inherited this team, I was thrilled. After all, I had a ton of respect for each individual on the team, and so did the folks within their functional silos. Maybe they weren't working well together as an executive team, but I naïvely believed that given all the challenges of running a business, making this group of talented individuals a cohesive team would be the easy part. That never happened. I had assigned too much value to team members' intelligence, pedigree, and functional expertise, and assigned too little value in how committed they were to being a high-functioning leadership team.

The lesson I learned is that valuing "the how" transcends "the what." Intelligence, pedigree, and functional expertise are table stakes. Successfully leading an organization hinges on the way the leadership team members engage, communicate, and support one another.

Eventually, making the necessary changes to that team proved to be painful because I truly liked and respected each member. But it also provided an opportunity to rebuild a team that was truly committed to a defined set of behaviors and values, and to forming relationships built on trust, transparency, alignment, and accountability. The advantage this brings to an organization—when the leadership team is running in the same direction with purpose and energy—can't be overstated. Prioritizing and reinforcing these behaviors fosters a resilient and cohesive team that can navigate challenges with collective strength. I'm blessed today to be working with a truly unified leadership team, and the trickle-down impact to the rest of the organization has been extremely positive.

When that same consultant from the off-site recently asked me if I would enthusiastically rehire every member of my current executive team, my answer was an emphatic *yes*. If you can say the same, great. If not, and if you don't think you can get them there, I suggest you move swiftly to build the team that you and your organization need.

MISTAKE #5

Failing at Feedback

*Withholding feedback is
choosing comfort over growth.*

—Adam Grant

FAILING AT FEEDBACK

G iving and receiving feedback is tough and uncomfortable. That's why most leaders and their teams don't do it very well, if at all.

When my peers from The Table Group and I work with teams, we do a pre-event assessment proprietary to The Table Group, known creatively as the Team Assessment. It is based on Lencioni's best-known and best-selling book, *The Five Dysfunctions of a Team*. The five dysfunctions in order are:

> Absence of Trust
> Fear of Conflict
> Lack of Commitment
> Avoidance of Accountability
> Inattention to Results

The first time we work with a team, almost without exception, the lowest score concerns that fourth dysfunction: Avoidance of Accountability. And giving and receiving feedback fits squarely in that category.

That practice is so important, in fact, that at the end of our first off-site with an executive team, my peers and I run an exercise called

Team Effectiveness: Everyone on the team shares, in front of the group, one specific behavioral item each team member does well that they should keep doing, followed by one specific behavior they could improve upon. As we explain this exercise, most people have a look on their faces that suggests they wish they had not come back after the last break. The exercise is raw and a bit uncomfortable at first because most of us are not used to giving honest, direct feedback to one another, especially in front of a group.

But if done in the spirit of making the team better, while keeping in mind that feedback is a gift, this approach to peer-to-peer feedback is extremely powerful. When I first encountered this exercise 10 years ago at our own off-site, four of my five Table Group peers gave me constructive feedback along these lines: "You know, Mike, sometimes you might want to think before you speak."

Four out of five!

I thanked them and called my wife that night to share the story and the feedback.

"I've been telling you that for *20 years!*" she responded. "But your peers share that you need to think before you speak, and *now* you want to work on it?"

Honest, direct, peer-to-peer feedback—on both the giving and the receiving end—is difficult without practice, but very powerful. And it's common among great teams.

But why is giving and receiving feedback so difficult? We know that we need to do it, that our people deserve it, and that regular, direct feedback will make the team better. Think about those best teams you have ever been a part of; in most instances they were marked by honest and direct feedback, both when things went well and when they didn't. We all learned the importance of feedback early on, perhaps even as kids. In fact, my kids' sports teams provide great examples.

My daughter, Elena, played point guard for her high school; on a competitive club basketball team that traveled the United States; and then at Whitman College, making it to the NCAA tournament in each of her four years at the school. Her coaches gave brutally honest feedback—the criticisms were instant and intense. But my daughter not only took that direct feedback from her coaches, she also gave it repeatedly in her roles as floor general and/or team captain. And she and her teammates gave and received feedback from one another throughout the game in order to perform at their best and get what they all wanted: a win.

My son, Jack, was a passionate lacrosse player during his high school years in Boise, an up-and-coming lacrosse hub with new teams being launched every month. During the year he started playing, the city went from 14 teams to 104! But lacrosse is not easy to understand without clear coaching and guidance. Cradling, for instance, is an important skill, but the technique takes time to master, and direct feedback is critical to getting it right. And hitting another player with your stick (something both primal and innate in every boy I have ever known) is legal but must be done in a certain way to avoid time in the penalty box. Kids new to the sport need constant feedback—not only from their coaches, but also from their more experienced teammates—if they are to learn the game and find success on the field.

My 16-year-old, Gabs, who favors soccer, receives and gives feedback regularly on her high school and traveling club soccer teams.

She and her teammates have specific practice and seasonal goals as well as in-game strategies and plays they must execute in order to secure victory. When they are successful, they celebrate together, but when they fail, they give feedback as to what could have gone better, to make sure they don't repeat those same mistakes. How else will they get better and reinforce their winning culture?

All this seems to make sense on a field or court of play. But on a leadership or work team, for some reason it seems harder. It's not easy telling your employees or a colleague that their performance could have been better and how they might improve. Or telling your boss how he or she might have done things differently for the good of the team. Or asking someone who works for you to share what you might do better as a leader. And yet we've seen continually that this is exactly what must happen for a leadership team and its organization to thrive.

As leaders, we must be willing to provide honest and direct feedback, sometimes publicly and at other times privately, both when things go right and when they go wrong. As leaders, we must also insist our people give one another clear, candid feedback. And perhaps most important, we must be willing to solicit feedback ourselves.

FAILING TO PROVIDE RECOGNITION

Sanjay Mehrotra, President and CEO, Micron Technology, Inc.

Soon after I joined Micron as CEO in 2017, I pulled my executive team together in Half Moon Bay, California, for a two-day off-site. Although I had spent time with everyone on the senior leadership team individually and the team had been together as a full group for various meetings, I wanted to make sure we spent some extended time together in the first 90 days of my tenure. If the company was going to grow and succeed in achieving its lofty goals, this team would need to become a *great* team, and we needed to do it quickly. To get there, I knew the members of the team had to get to know one another better. We had to become aligned both behaviorally and intellectually.

During the second day of the event, we had a discussion about the organization's core values, with the intention of communicating those values across the enterprise in the weeks ahead. As we worked together to finalize those core values, we went through an exercise where we individually thought of one person in the organization who was a great fit at Micron, someone who we would enthusiastically rehire—and if we could find more people just like them, we would hire them, too, as fast as we could. Then we listed the qualities that made that person such a great fit. We took turns sharing with the rest of the group the names and characteristics of those we had listed.

As we wrapped up the exercise, we commented on how several people had been named multiple times in the exercise. One person's name was shared *four* different times. Our company has more than

30,000 employees! The consultant asked if the people on the list, especially those listed multiple times, were told often enough how important they were to the company.

It got quiet in the conference room.

My executive team is made up of extremely smart, analytical leaders who move fast and push hard to make sure we reach our organizational goals. As with many senior leaders in technology (and in other industries, I suspect), we often move quickly to what's next, which means we often fail to slow down enough to celebrate success—or to thank the people in our organization when they do great things. I have been guilty of this too many times in my career, in spite of having great intentions to be better at this type of recognition.

I do take pride in giving direct, real-time feedback, and I have developed a reputation throughout my career for "telling it like it is" in individual conversations, team meetings, and presentations. I learned this first from my father, who was an extremely direct, driven man. He had high expectations, and if any of my three siblings or I needed constructive criticism, he was never shy about providing it.

I carried my father's ways into my career both at Intel—where the culture of *disagree and commit* reinforces it—and then at SanDisk, where I was a cofounder and CEO. The cultural diversity of the executive leadership team there led to a culture of feedback, honesty, and productive conflict. If I am honest with myself, though, I am more apt to offer that direct feedback when things go wrong or don't meet my expectations than when they go well.

This is something I knew I couldn't afford to have happen

going forward at Micron. As CEO of the organization, I need to continually find better ways to give proactive, positive feedback, because it starts with me—and needs to cascade throughout my executive team.

And it did, in fact, start with me right then and there, at the off-site in Half Moon Bay. I picked up the phone and called the employee who had been named by four different executives: Naga is his name.

When he answered, I put him on the speaker so we all could hear. "Naga, this is Sanjay," I said. "The senior executive team just went through a group exercise where we listed employees who align perfectly to our core values. Your name was mentioned several times, by several different leaders, so we thought we'd call you as a group to make sure you know how valuable you are to the company. Thank you for all your great work and for exhibiting our values, the behaviors that make our company a great one."

Then the executive team spontaneously broke out in applause and cheers, expressing the meaning and emotion behind our effort to recognize an employee and his great work.

That call, which took about three minutes, was a small, simple gesture that had real impact on a great employee. I learned later that Naga really appreciated it and told his family it was a call he would never forget. It's not every day that the entire executive team of the company calls, out of the blue, to thank you.

Part of being both a high-performing and healthy organization is having an engaged workforce, and a big part of that is making sure employees are appropriately recognized and appreciated for their great efforts. As leaders, we can't make the mistake of assuming good people know their value. That needs to be demonstrated first by a company's executive leaders—as we strive to do at Micron—by taking ownership and accepting personal responsibility for making sure the company recognizes great work, giving feedback when things go well, and celebrating our successes.

FAILING TO DEMAND DIFFICULT CONVERSATIONS

Brian Smith, Partner, Gemstone Capital; Co-Owner, Ada Sand and Gravel, Inc.; Principal DEANCO Management Group, Inc.

"Hey, Brian, do you have a minute? There is something I'd like to talk to you about . . . *privately*." The question came from one of my direct reports. I'll call him Ian.

I've always been a fan of the open-door policy, and over the course of my career as a leader up to that point, I took any and all impromptu meetings ever requested. Good leaders do that, right? I had appreciated the individual time previous managers had spent with me throughout my career, and my sense was that the best leaders practiced this policy. They took the extra one-on-one time to listen to their people and solve the problems those people faced with respect to their work.

As he entered my office for our one-on-one, Ian closed my door—making it a closed-door meeting as a result of an open-door policy. Funny.

Ian had two things he wanted to share with me. The first was a business issue related to a struggle he was having with a supplier. He felt he had made a mistake and wanted to share it with me, but not in front of the team. This was something I had seen multiple times before, in fact, with this very same supplier, and I had a pretty good idea how to solve it.

The second thing on his mind concerned an issue with a colleague and was going to be a bit harder to solve. People issues, I have found, are usually trickier, and this was no exception. As Ian explained the situation, I could see that it was a highly charged, emotional issue with another one of my directs. Let's call him Brett.

What I should have done in this situation was to force Ian and Brett to have a hard conversation and share their feelings directly with one another. But I didn't, and that turned out to be a time-wasting mistake—one I had made countless times before. In fact, I had made this same mistake with these *same two* leaders multiple times in the past. Each time they had "issues," I would take their individual meetings; then I would listen and act as a sounding board for one or both of them *separately*, so I could then make some suggestions to remedy the situation. Occasionally, I would even go back and forth between them, again separately, to help them come to a resolution.

What I found over time was that their relationship never got better, and that I was a big part of the problem. The two of them coming to me separately improved *my* relationship with each leader, but the relationship between *them* continued to suffer. Their issues not only kept them from establishing a good relationship, but it was distracting them and others from their work. Handling their issues individually took hours and hours—time that was better spent elsewhere.

When I finally realized my mistake—that I could have avoided this loss easily by having them give one another feedback directly and work it out on their own—I pulled them together for a three-way, admittedly difficult, conversation and told them I would no longer be available for these separate meetings. They would need to talk through issues they were having together first. Then, if there was no resolution, they could come to me *together*, and I would make the final call.

With respect to the business issue Ian mentioned, I can say I handled that one better, at least this time. Having heard and addressed that same vendor issue several months before, I knew I had made a mistake when it was originally brought up, by not forcing a group conversation the first time. This time, though, after giving Ian my initial thoughts, I asked him to share his mistake with our weekly team meeting—where another team member, I'll call him John, acknowledged that he had made a similar error with a different vendor.

Bringing up the issue in front of the group meant everyone could benefit and learn from the conversation. Moreover, the team came up with a better solution than I was going to suggest during my private conversation with Ian. The team also had an opportunity to see that being vulnerable and sharing a mistake is a great way to make the team better. Bringing this important conversation in front of the group helped the team right away and also would save time down the road in similar situations.

Having been through these experiences and others like them over my years as a leader, I always look for ways to force difficult and important conversations between members of my team. Those hard conversations build relationships; make the team more cohesive and most important, lead to better business results.

FAILING TO SHARE THE KIND TRUTH

Brett Robinson, President, Sparrow Living

"I don't think you're working very hard, Brett."

That was the start to a difficult conversation I had been both expecting and dreading for over a year. My manager was right, and I wondered if my behavior was going to cost me my day job or just provoke a stern reprimand. I deserved the former, but I was hoping for the latter.

I had always dreamed of being a sportscaster, which is not uncommon for a young man who grew up in the Chicago area playing and watching sports every free waking hour. Talking about sports all day and getting paid for it? Are you kidding me? What's not to like about that? So when the opportunity presented itself to moonlight at two stations in Santa Barbara, California (including the one where Jim Rome began his storied career!), I jumped at it. I put a great deal of my energy into those evening and weekend opportunities instead of my day job, selling for a large consumer products company. After all, who grows up dreaming of being a consumer products salesman?

My manager was clear in that conversation, both about my sub-par performance and about his expectations moving forward. While he was very kind to mention that I had great potential, he was clear about his opinion that I was selling myself short.

I'm certain he didn't enjoy that conversation. For that matter, neither did I. But he was direct and fair in his assessment, and I left with clarity as to where I stood and what I needed to do. I got off easier than I deserved that day, and as uncomfortable as it was to get that feedback, I appreciated it.

In fact, that feedback lit a fire under me. I doubled down on my sales efforts, and that hard work produced great results. That conversation was a pivotal moment that launched an extremely rewarding sales career that has lasted 35 years. It was also a key learning moment for me—one that I have been able to apply as a leader and manager. Although I question why it took so long (an entire year!) for my manager to have that difficult conversation with me, to his credit, he did it in the end. By now, I have worked with and for enough leaders in my career to know that avoiding difficult conversations is all too common, even among the best leaders.

Patrick Lencioni speaks to this responsibility in his book *The Motive*, listing "having uncomfortable and difficult conversations" as a first of five responsibilities that even the best leaders often abdicate or delegate. Whether listing it first means it is the most common or most important, I don't know—but it is the one that resonates with me the most, and the one I have struggled with the most over my years as a leader.

Although I am far from perfect at having these conversations, and I often dread (and have even lost sleep over) the most difficult ones, I have gotten better at them over time. That's because I have learned a few lessons during hundreds of these hard conversations over my 30-plus years as a leader. Here are some of them:

- *Timing matters.* I have found that sooner is almost always better when giving behavioral feedback. Early in my career I waited until a performance review cycle to give the most difficult and uncomfortable feedback. This is a bad idea and bad management form. Waiting as long as six months (or even 12!) to let someone know about a behavior that is worthy of feedback is both irresponsible and cruel. I can still see the face of one of the employees after I held back on offering feedback until his performance review. *You let me do that wrong for six months and didn't tell me? Shame on you!* is what his face conveyed. And his face was right. Sooner is almost always better, both for the receiver of the feedback and for the giver.

• *Share the kind truth.* I have heard it said that in having hard conversations, giving feedback is sharing the kind truth. Note the two words here: kind *and* true. I remember a hard conversation with a young saleswoman on my team, letting her know that the squeaky little mouse voice she used when excited didn't sound professional—and was costing her credibility and probably sales. In that instance I was 50 percent on kind and true: There was no kindness in my words. She cried, and I felt awful. Now, almost 30 years later, I still regret that harsher-than-necessary tone to the conversation.

• *Have pure intentions.* When I am taking too long to have a hard conversation, I always try to stop and ask myself if my intentions are pure. Am I avoiding the conversation because I want to feel better about myself? Is it because I crave harmony? Is it because I want the employee to like me and don't want to risk being unpopular? I have been guilty of all of these reasons over the years. If your intentions are pure and designed with the employee's development and the company's best interests in mind, avoiding the hard conversation is rarely the answer.

I'm glad I didn't end up pursuing that broadcasting career. Although sports are still a big part of my life, I am much more passionate about developing people, enabling their success, and seeing them achieve great things. I am confident that a career in broadcasting would not have allowed me that same opportunity.

And although I still don't love having those difficult and uncomfortable conversations, I know they are something I need to continue to do, and continue to get better at, if I am going to continue to be the best leader I can be.

FAILING TO TAKE OWNERSHIP AND DEFINE ROLES

René Lacerte, CEO and Founder, BILL

One thing of many I love about my wife, Joyce, is that she can be very direct. For example, she had no trouble saying what should have been obvious to me: "You know you're getting fired, right?"

Fired? No, I didn't know that. But I agreed it *was* a bit odd that the board chair of the company where I was CEO had just called and asked me to meet with the board first thing the next morning.

Another thing I love about my wife is that her experience as a venture capitalist was broad and her instincts were dead-on, and this was no exception. That was indeed the reason for the meeting.

I can point to several factors that led to that outcome, including slowing growth, a poorly aligned three-headed leadership team (fashionable in the late 1990s—but only temporarily, for good reason), and a lack of clearly defined roles and responsibilities for the three of us on that team. Ultimately, that led to this conversation in November 2004, when the board asked me to step down as CEO and become CFO.

I knew why: I had failed as CEO to take accountability for the company's challenges and then move quickly to solve them. That morning in the boardroom, I asked for more time to address our challenges and prove my ability to turn things around, but it was too late; the board had made its decision. I became CFO, hired my replacement, and worked hard to clean up the confusion I had indirectly created.

That day, I learned a painful but important lesson.

Clarity of roles and responsibilities on an executive team is important for a number of reasons, but perhaps the most important one is to avoid diffusion of responsibility. If everyone is responsible, no one is. Without clarity on who is doing what and who is accountable for what, the buck stops . . . nowhere. Confusion across the organization, the chaos of office politics, missed opportunities, and poor results are bound to follow.

Throughout my life, music has often spoken to me as a way to frame my thoughts, and a song comes to mind here: Michael Jackson's "Man in the Mirror." I doubt Michael was thinking about high-tech executive teams and role clarity when he wrote it, but the concept definitely applies. After I was fired as the CEO, I had to look myself in the mirror and examine what I had done (and importantly, *not* done) that resulted in our company's challenges and ultimately my demotion. I knew I would need to "change my ways" the next time around.

With that lesson in mind, 18 months later I started BILL.com (now BILL) and was very deliberate in not taking on any cofounders. I wanted to make sure that it was clear to me that I was the CEO—the primary person responsible for big decisions and ultimately the success of the business. Missed results? My responsibility. Poor hire on the executive team? That's on me. In short, all roads led to me. My personal commitment and accountability to our mission of "helping small and medium-sized businesses thrive" sets the tone for the entire company. Ultimately, I am accountable to our board, our investors, and the SMBs that are our customers.

As the company has grown, I have deliberately passed key responsibilities and accountabilities to others on our executive team, or eTeam. I have been painstakingly clear with respect not only to what eTeam roles are, but what their accountabilities and responsibilities are as well. As an example, after promoting our CFO to the role of president *and* CFO, I recently made the decision to remove myself from the eTeam meetings as he created his own rhythm. I love the members of that team and missed being in those meetings, but I needed to make sure there was no confusion as to whose meeting it was now and who had ultimate operational responsibility for the business and the operations he now leads.

Over the past 25 years, I have learned that accountability for a team is set by the leader. It is essential that, as the CEO, I continuously define and lead through accountability at every stage of the company. I have also learned that as that definition changes for me, it is super important to acknowledge the changes so the team can lean in and support that evolution. I may have learned this the hard way, but I am grateful I did.

FAILING TO GIVE IMMEDIATE FEEDBACK

Kamal Aggarwal, Executive Vice President, National Semiconductor Corporation, LSI Logic, Fairchild Semiconductor (retired)

By the time I became the executive vice president at National Semiconductor, one of the world's leading semiconductor manufacturers, I had rightly earned the reputation of being a hard-ass. My colleagues and many in the technology industry knew that I was a straight shooter who always spoke the truth—no sugarcoating, ever.

Early in my career, all too frequently I saw a leadership error that I knew I couldn't allow myself to make: Many leaders avoided confrontation by allowing stage-managed results—results that were for show and that hid problems and challenges in the business. These so-called leaders seldom encouraged bad news. They also failed to offer direct, immediate feedback to someone who was making a mistake, doing something that hurt the company, or failing to keep their commitments.

I saw this happen over and over. Leaders either were afraid to make waves, cared more about their popularity than about company results, or planned to provide input at a later time—a time that never came. Consequently, results were subpar. If you don't demand accountability, you get what you are willing to accept.

It became clear to me that this was not the way a good leader leads, and I was unwilling to repeat that same mistake. I had given my team one battle cry—reduce cycle time by 50 percent without sacrificing quality—and I needed them to ensure it happened. And they needed leaders who gave honest, immediate feedback if we were ever off track. They also needed to know that a culture that accepted the same failing practices and approaches, one that made excuses or ignored promises, would no longer be tolerated.

A good leader needs to provide immediate, direct feedback that would improve both the performance of the employee and the results of the company. This was my primary goal. In my opinion, it was why I was hired.

Soon after I took over as the executive vice president of worldwide operations, as I sat in a meeting with several other senior executives and the company plant managers, I saw that those managers were sheltering the executives from the truth of how the business was running. Things were not going well in the company, but executives were hearing a rosy tale that didn't match reality. This false perception was helping no one, and the managers' behavior was inhibiting the company from achieving its goals. The executive team needed to hear the honest, unfiltered truth—immediately—so that we could turn things around.

As one particular plant manager told his fable, I challenged him straight away, calling him out for his inaccurate information. This had not been a common practice at the company before my arrival, and the feedback—especially its public nature—was embarrassing to him. He called me afterward, quite angry, and asked that I not do that again, especially publicly.

I explained that if we were to become a high-performing organization, our culture would have to embrace direct, honest feedback up and down the organization. Furthermore, the public nature of that feedback was critical. Had I not called him and others out publicly in that meeting for misinformation, it would have implicitly condoned that behavior, which then would propagate across the organization and get in the way of our future success.

To his credit, he took the feedback to heart and made big changes with the approach to feedback across his part of the organization. His results improved, as did others' in the organization, as together we embraced this concept. It helped us achieve our singular goal that year: reducing cycle time by 50 percent without sacrificing quality.

A change to the culture had begun. It required honest, immediate, often public feedback—up, down, and across the organization. Cycle times improved, profits grew, employees started taking greater pride and held one another accountable, and our organization was better as a result.

FAILING TO REMAIN OPEN TO TEAM FEEDBACK

Dr. John Slattery, Founder, Slattery Orthodontics

I knew from the day I met Kathy that our working relationship was not going to work out.

I had moved back to my hometown after spending over a decade in school, earning three degrees at three different universities on the path required to become an orthodontist. Now I had been hired into a large group practice with three other doctors, and on that fateful first day I was assigned Kathy—and only Kathy—as my lead clinical assistant. She would be the one to help me manage my practice within the practice. In addition to the main location, the two of us were charged with starting up a satellite practice one day a week.

As we were introduced, we sized each other up. I had an image in my mind of my first employee—and she wasn't it. If I had a panel of 10 or 15 people to interview, I doubt she would have been my first choice, or even my second.

I remember someone at the office letting me know that Kathy had worked in orthodontics for a long time and probably already knew more than I did. Was that threatening to me, a newly minted orthodontist? You bet it was. We were peers in age. She had a quiet confidence about how to do things and wasn't afraid to point out a mistake or how things *should* be done. I had expected to be the superior in position but instead was feeling minimized and threatened by her.

I'm sure my body language said a lot that day. I remember thinking to myself, *The last thing I need is someone telling* me *how to run* my *practice.*

I couldn't have been more wrong.

In the previous 15 years, leading up to that first day, I had been at the bottom of a number of different hierarchies.

At Santa Clara University as an undergraduate, I studied mechanical engineering and every day was taught by professors telling me what I needed to know and giving honest guidance and feedback when I did something wrong. But I was learning a process and learning the practical ways to someday be an engineer.

I was also on the crew team, so every morning at 5 a.m. I got on the water and listened to my coaches and coxswains (110-pound tyrants of the vessel who watched my every move alongside the other oarsmen) happily screaming at me when my timing was off. The idea was that this immediate, honest feedback would help us achieve the elusive "swing" (akin to being *in the zone* in other sports) and avoid having to give up our shirts to our competitors in our next race—a humbling but motivating tradition in that sport. Again, I was learning a process, the practical application of which would result in better times and, hopefully, races won.

After graduation, I spent a few years working for Andersen Consulting. In that business, there were clear roles and reporting relationships, and I was at the bottom of the org chart as a new consultant. The company was known for its set of systems and processes, and I needed to learn them and conform to them. I was subservient to the managers, senior leaders, and partners, who knew more than I did and often told me, without my input, what assignments I would be taking on and in which city I would live for each assignment. With greater experience and knowledge, they would direct my work, critique my approaches and the quality of my work, and show me the proven processes and practical approaches regarding how to be successful in client interactions.

Although I worked hard and found success in these different environments, I found I wasn't fulfilled in my career choice. With some great guidance from a friend's parent who was a college counselor, I chose a very different path: attending dental school in California and orthodontic school in Pennsylvania. Once again, smarter and more knowledgeable people were telling me what I was—and wasn't—doing well. Looking over my shoulder in clinics and labs, my professors offered constant and critical feedback to get me where I needed to be as a professional and a successful clinical practitioner in my trade.

After 15 years as the lowest-ranked and least important person, the one who always *received* the feedback and had to do as others directed, I graduated from ortho school. Earning that diploma made me feel that something had finally changed: I should be the leader in all aspects of my practice. I had earned the degree. I had all the appropriate clinical knowledge and training. Now I was ready to be *the man*, the one in charge, and the one sole leader of my practice.

The problem with this, though, was that I was not skilled or experienced in actually *running* a practice. I knew the anatomy of the mouth, the mechanics of braces, the techniques, the angles, the tools that were necessary for fixing crooked teeth, overbites, and underbites. But I didn't know the practical components of running a successful practice. Finances, billing, suppliers, appointment systems, patient flow—these were the practical things I hadn't learned in school but desperately needed to do well if my practice was going to succeed.

I suspect this is true for many rookie leaders—wanting to prove themselves as the one in charge and desiring to demonstrate their knowledge, competence, and smarts. When image and pride are given too much importance, these leaders are less open to ideas and insights—to the feedback on how to do things and the strategies needed for success. It takes vulnerability to admit you need help, and I think vulnerability is especially difficult for doctors and new leaders—or in my case, both.

As Kathy and I worked together, over time I came to recognize and appreciate her as a second key leader who was committed to the practice and shared my top priority: providing great care for our patients. When I allowed myself to be vulnerable and admitted to needing help from Kathy (let's face it, probably more than she needed me), our working relationship improved. When I got over myself and opened up to her wise counsel on the mechanics and the important systems and processes for running the business, our business improved, too.

Seeing Kathy as a threat had been a mistake, the product of a closed mind. By finally opening up to her crucial contributions, I gained the opportunity to focus on and use my key strengths, and I trusted Kathy to use hers in support of our growing practice.

In fact, when I decided to leave that first partnership to start my own business, Kathy came with me, and we launched the practice together. By taking advantage of the two distinct sets of skills and leveraging each of our strengths, we were able to create a successful new business. I recall the body language was much better on *that* first day.

Kathy and I have now been working together for over 25 years. She still gives me honest, direct feedback, such as when we designed the building for our growing practice, when she has an idea for how to improve a system or process, or when there is a booger in my nose or broccoli in my teeth. (None of the nearly 70 patients I see in a given day want to see that!) Her direct feedback to me on these and other things results in a better work environment, happier employees, better care for our patients, and ultimately a better, healthier business.

FAILING TO SOLICIT FEEDBACK

Taavo Godtfredsen, Cofounder, Advantage CEO; CEO Advisor and Executive Coach

I like to think I am a pretty good husband and father. Then again, a 2017 study (described in the *Forbes* article "Only 15% of People Are Self-Aware—Here's How to Change") indicates that about 95 percent of people *think* they are self-aware when only 10 percent to 15 percent truly are. So, as someone who is passionate about feedback, I thought I would check my self-assessment and ask my family for an honest, direct response.

"How am I doing as a father and husband?" I asked each member of my family in individual conversations. "And what's one thing I could do better?" Of course, believing I was in the self-aware group, I expected there would be no surprises. Wrong!

I was happy that the whole family responded similarly to the first question and gave me a passing grade, but their responses to the second were very different. My wife responded that chipping in a bit more with some household tasks like garbage and recycling would be much appreciated. Fair criticism, and something I could absolutely do better.

My daughter had no comment on what I could improve upon when I asked a first time, but when I was persistent and asked again, she told me that I could be more patient and not raise my voice as much. *Ouch.* Didn't see that one coming. I recognized the humor in my impatience when waiting for her response and thanked her for the constructive criticism. I agreed it was something I could do better as a father, and chalked it up to something common that a lot of parents need to improve on.

My son's feedback was more immediate—and much more painful to hear. "Dad," he said, "you always interrupt me. You never let me finish what I am saying." *Double ouch.* That one really hurt, and I felt horrible. The last thing I want my son to feel is that I am not listening to him and valuing what he is sharing with me. Talk about a parental blind spot—I had no idea I was doing this to him. But it was true: I would interrupt him sometimes, thinking I knew what he was going to say. Listening, as I have always felt strongly, is what great parents and leaders do.

Having acknowledged and thanked each family member for their feedback, I knew I had taken a good first step. But if this experience was going to be truly meaningful, if I was going to improve as a husband, father, and leader of my most important team, I knew I would have to not just listen and thank them, but also make those changes to my behavior.

Feedback is the muscle behind continuous improvement. The idea behind feedback is really quite simple: How can we improve if we don't know how we are doing? As leaders, don't we want to model improvement and growth for our followers and demonstrate courage and humility? This is why I believe asking for feedback is the single biggest way a leader can have an impact on their organization. Now that's a bold statement to make! And a number of the CEOs I have coached over the years have asked me to back it up.

While there is a wealth of data to support my position, one 2015 study by Zenger/Folkman (described in another *Forbes* article, "The Question That Improves Effectiveness") supported it especially well. Leveraging a database of more than 22,000 leaders and the 360-degree assessments they completed, the leadership development firm took one item, "This person asks for and acts on feedback from others," to see how it correlated with a composite score for all of the items in their assessment. This is what they discovered:

- Leaders in the top 10th percentile on "asks for and acts on feedback" were ranked in the 90th percentile of overall leadership effectiveness.

- Leaders in the 66th to 90th percentile on "asks for and acts on feedback" were ranked in the 71st percentile of overall leadership effectiveness.

- Leaders in the bottom 10th percentile on "asks for and acts on feedback" were ranked in the 12th percentile of overall leadership effectiveness.

Having worked with and interviewed hundreds of CEOs and executive leaders over the past two decades, my own qualitative research supports the importance of leaders asking for feedback as well: Multiple senior executives I have coached have made significant strides in their overall effectiveness and business outcomes, as reported by their peers and direct reports, after asking for feedback and taking action on that feedback. One of the most successful CEOs I have ever coached, for example, sent out a survey to the entire organization asking for feedback on his strengths (to amplify) and areas for improvement (to fix). Of course, when you ask for feedback, you set the expectation that you will do something with it—especially if you ask for it from all of your employees globally! This CEO did not disappoint. He first provided all of the employees with a summary of what he learned via video, approximately a week after sending the survey. He began the video perfectly, starting with "Everyone in the company gets a performance review, [so] why shouldn't I?" He then methodically laid out his own performance plan for the coming year based on their input. This is what great leaders do. They don't preach about the importance of feedback; they model it. In this case, the CEO did it in the most powerful way possible.

When the most senior leaders ask for feedback regularly, it sets the tone for other leaders to do the same and leads to continuous improvement for the whole organization. In many cases, people do what people see. It can be that simple!

Also, by asking for feedback, a leader shows vulnerability, which allows others in his or her organization to do the same. This creates an environment of openness, sharing of ideas, and debate, and allows for better decisions and ultimately better organizational success.

I'll close with a simple question: What if every leader in your organization made a commitment to asking for feedback regularly and worked hard to change behaviors that the feedback recommended?

My own answer would be that your leaders would be more effective, business results would be more easily achieved, and your organizations would be stronger and healthier.

And those who are willing to apply that same approach at home would see better results there, too, which I am working to achieve as we speak.

CONCLUSION

I have been called a lot of things in my life.

Dad, *Father*, and *Daddy* are three of my favorites—three different names for the same role, used by my three kids. I'm not sure why, but my kids are all very different, and when they address me that way, even when it's to ask me for some cash, I love it.

My wife calls me a variety of things: *Hubby*, *Darlin'*, *Lover*, and *Willis* (when I make that certain face—*Watchu talkin' 'bout, Willis?*) are some of the ones I like best from her. She has more colorful names for me as well.

Other favorites over the course of my 57 years include *friend*, *uncle*, *buddy*, *amigo*, and *neighbor*, as well as a number of titles I have been honored to be called: *leader*, *manager*, *boss*, *elder*, *captain*, and *coach*.

One thing I haven't been called as often as I'd like to report, though, is *vulnerable*. This has been a challenge for me over the course of my life, especially in my roles as a leader.

I started this book talking about my first role as a leader and some of the damaging mistakes I made. In the story, I blamed the lack of guidance and lack of mentoring, and that definitely was part of it. But my own lack of humility and the arrogance I showed, especially in those first leadership roles, probably had even more to do with my many failures.

I know I'm not alone in being challenged in this area as a leader, but the truth is that the very best leaders I have known and worked with are exactly that: vulnerable. They demonstrate it daily by saying things like *I'm sorry* or *I blew it* or *Help me* or *I'm not very good at this*. And when they admit their mistakes openly and honestly, the members of their teams and others in their organizations follow their lead. When leaders "go first" this way, their people can be more vulnerable as well, trust improves, and the team gets better. For great examples of vulnerability, you need not look any farther than the 35 stories in the pages of this book, where remarkable leaders admit to mistakes for the whole world to see. And for that, I'm both in awe and forever grateful to them.

In the final mistake documented in this book, Taavo Godtfredsen shared that a leader's ability to solicit feedback and then act on that feedback is so critical. I wholeheartedly agree, and I saved his story for last for a reason: Asking for raw, critical feedback is the ultimate demonstration of vulnerability. But the willingness to ask for it and then act upon it ends up making leaders better, teams better, and organizations better. Its importance can't be overstated.

So, with feedback in mind, I offer a challenge in wrapping up this book: In the spirit of vulnerability and *asking* for feedback, I challenge you to self-assess your strengths and weaknesses related to the mistakes shared in this book.

In addition to the in-book self-assessment on the following pages, the assessment is available via downloadable PDF on my website: mikemchargueconsulting.com. Assessing yourself and talking to the members of your team for their feedback is a great and vulnerable step to take toward improving yourself and your team.

I wish you all the best as a leader. May you be vulnerable, ask for feedback, and learn from your mistakes as the best leaders do.

LEADER SELF-ASSESSMENT

———

The following five pages contain a short self-assessment on each of the five mistake categories discussed in *That's on Me*: confusion, connection, meetings, hiring/firing, and feedback. In each, please rate yourself as you believe your team members would rate you, by choosing the appropriate number from the 1-5 scale below. The assessment is designed to increase awareness related to your strengths and development areas as a leader and provide a foundation for meaningful conversations for you and your team. (This assessment is also available online at mikemchargueconsulting.com.)

Lousy	Needing to improve	OK	Pretty Good	Outstanding
1	2	3	4	5

At the bottom of each assessment, tally your total score. Then see how your total score matches up to the rating below.

5-9	10-14	15-19	20-22	23+
This is a real challenge for you and, therefore, for your team.	You have some work to do here.	Not bad—but do you really want to be an average leader?	You are on your way to greatness.	This is a real strength for you.

CONFUSION SELF-ASSESSMENT

Lousy	Needing to improve	OK	Pretty Good	Outstanding
1	2	3	4	5

DO I ALLOW CONFUSION ON MY TEAM?

My team would say...   **Score: 1-5**

1. I am _____ at communicating the company's purpose.	
2. I am _____ at communicating the company's values.	
3. I am _____ at communicating the company's and team's goals.	
4. I am _____ at communicating the company's and team's priorities.	
5. I am _____ at continuously communicating and reinforcing the most important things in our business.	
Total Confusion Score	

5–9	10–14	15–19	20–22	23+
This is a real challenge for you and, therefore, for your team.	You have some work to do here.	Not bad—but do you really want to be an average leader?	You are on your way to greatness.	This is a real strength for you.

CONNECTION SELF-ASSESSMENT

Lousy	Needing to improve	OK	Pretty Good	Outstanding
1	2	3	4	5

DO I FAIL TO CONNECT WITH MY TEAM?

My team would say...   **Score: 1-5**

1. I am _____ at being open and vulnerable.	
2. I am _____ at getting to know the members of the team.	
3. I am _____ at listening.	
4. I am _____ at giving the right amount of guidance and support (not too much and not too little) for the team to succeed.	
5. I am _____ at expressing gratitude.	
Total Connection Score	

5-9	10-14	15-19	20-22	23+
This is a real challenge for you and, therefore, for your team.	You have some work to do here.	Not bad—but do you really want to be an average leader?	You are on your way to greatness.	This is a real strength for you.

MEETINGS SELF-ASSESSMENT

Lousy	Needing to improve	OK	Pretty Good	Outstanding
1	2	3	4	5

DO I RUN TRULY AWFUL MEETINGS?

My team would say...　　　　　　　　　　　　　　**Score: 1-5**

1. I am _____ at starting meetings with clarity.	
2. I am _____ at aligning our meetings to what's most important.	
3. I am _____ at allowing for productive conflict in our meetings.	
4. I am _____ at ensuring clarity of decisions, commitments, and actions during meetings.	
5. I am _____ at ensuring we leave meetings with clear messaging.	
Total Meetings Score	

5-9	10-14	15-19	20-22	23+
This is a real challenge for you and, therefore, for your team.	You have some work to do here.	Not bad—but do you really want to be an average leader?	You are on your way to greatness.	This is a real strength for you.

HIRING/FIRING SELF-ASSESSMENT

Lousy	Needing to improve	OK	Pretty Good	Outstanding
1	2	3	4	5

DO I HIRE TOO FAST OR FIRE TOO SLOW?

My team would say...   **Score: 1-5**

1. I am _____ at hiring people aligned to the company's purpose.	
2. I am _____ at hiring people aligned to the company's values.	
3. I am _____ at hiring with alignment to cultural fit.	
4. I am _____ at taking the time necessary to get to know candidates before bringing them into the company.	
5. I am _____ at extracting poorly performing team members in a reasonable amount of time.	
Total Hiring/Firing Score	

5-9	10-14	15-19	20-22	23+
This is a real challenge for you and, therefore, for your team.	You have some work to do here.	Not bad—but do you really want to be an average leader?	You are on your way to greatness.	This is a real strength for you.

FEEDBACK SELF-ASSESSMENT

Lousy	Needing to improve	OK	Pretty Good	Outstanding
1	2	3	4	5

DO I FAIL TO GIVE AND SOLICIT FEEDBACK?

My team would say...   **Score: 1-5**

1. I am _____ at providing recognition for a job well done.	
2. I am _____ at giving honest and direct feedback when things could improve.	
3. I am _____ at giving immediate feedback.	
4. I am _____ at being open to hearing feedback from the team.	
5. I am _____ at soliciting feedback from the team and acting upon it.	
Total Feedback Score	

5-9	**10-14**	**15-19**	**20-22**	**23+**
This is a real challenge for you and, therefore, for your team.	You have some work to do here.	Not bad—but do you really want to be an average leader?	You are on your way to greatness.	This is a real strength for you.

ACKNOWLEDGMENTS

My amazing wife and editor, Anna, has been editing books—more than 350 of them at last count—for more than 35 years. And for 20 of those years, I talked to her about my desire to write a book, any book. While always encouraging, she continually shared with me that writing a book is not only difficult but requires long periods of focus and great attention to detail—definitely not my strengths. And as with most things, being an author is a lot easier when you've never been one, especially when you haven't even chosen a topic.

"Some people," she said, "simply aren't cut out for it."

I *knew* I was one of them, until I was struck by the notion that I not only have expert-level experience at making mistakes, but I also love talking to leaders about their mistakes and am passionate about helping them overcome them. I had my topic and began with vigor my journey toward being an author.

Whether large numbers of people would want to read it is another matter and remains to be seen, but it appears at least *you* did. So, thank you for that.

There are times you should listen to your wife; Anna's comments about how difficult it is to write a book turned out to be true. Not only was it difficult, but it also required the proverbial village to make it happen. I am so grateful to the hundreds of executives who shared the stories of their mistakes with me and their teams, and especially so to the 35 who were vulnerable enough to work with me and allow me to share their stories here.

My team of book people included my Run MMC Team: Molly Hamilton, who always keeps our business's wheels on; Amy Hoppock, who kept the wheels on this book project; and Mark Traylor, who has helped me keep my wheels on personally and spiritually for over 20 years. Your friendship and excitement for this book and our business seem never-ending, and I am honored to lead our best team. And to my highly detailed proofreader, Anita Stephens, who finds things that everyone else should have found. I also am grateful to my publisher, Greenleaf Publishing, and to their highly competent team, for helping me bring this book to life.

Thanks so much to my friends and colleagues at The Table Group. I'm especially grateful to Patrick Lencioni and Jeff Gibson, who graciously mentored me as I worked to craft my skills in the profession that feels like home. To Al Amador and David Ross who took me under their collective wing as I started and built my business—I'm forever grateful for your guidance. And to my principal consultant comrades, especially in our 7UP Pod—your collaboration, friendship, ideas, and feedback are so appreciated.

I'm a believer that iron sharpens iron, and I'm grateful to be surrounded in my life by some seriously heavy metal—in particular, the Braly Boys, the Power Five, the TVLG, the 100 Men for Good Advisory Board, and also my colleagues at EO Idaho, all of whom sharpen me in different ways.

I'm so very thankful for my super-supportive family, starting with Anna, who was the glue that held this project (and me!) together from start to finish. I love you, darlin'—you are my true companion and *SS!* I also want to thank my three amazing kids, Elena, Jack, and Gabs, who suffered greatly in having to hear idea after idea at dinner each night and on vacations and first thing in the morning and last thing at night. And I would be nowhere without my parents, Lanita Allen and Mike McHargue, and my stepmom, Liz McHargue. Your love and support of me and my crazy dreams are something I can never thank you enough for, and I try to pay forward with my own kids.

And finally, to Jesus, the ultimate example of vulnerability. He truly is the first and the last on this list.

ABOUT THE AUTHOR

Mike McHargue is the president and owner of Mike McHargue Consulting and a principal consultant with The Table Group, a Patrick Lencioni company. Mike helps leaders master the disciplines of organizational health so that their organizations can be more successful and their people can be more fulfilled in their work. His enterprise clients include the Mayo Clinic, Applied Materials, Carnival Corporation, Mutual of Omaha, St. Luke's Health System, Intel, Micron Technologies, Pacific Life, VISA, Lenovo, and World Vision.

Mike lives in Boise, Idaho, with his wife, Anna, and their three children, Elena, Jack, and Gabriella. When not making his own mistakes as a leader, he can be found running the Boise Foothills and Greenbelt or planning a next travel adventure.

For more information regarding Mike and his work, contact him at mike.mchargue@tablegroupconsulting.com, follow him on LinkedIn, or visit his webpage at mikemchargueconsulting.com.